OLD GLASS

OLD GLASS

MANUFACTURE · STYLES · USES

By

O. N. WILKINSON

LONDON · ERNEST BENN LIMITED

First published 1968 by Ernest Benn Limited
Bouverie House · Fleet Street · London · EC4

© *O. N. Wilkinson 1968*

Printed in Great Britain

510–06201–6

Contents

Illustrations

22 A clear green ewer with wrythen body. About A.D. 200. Found in Scotland

23 Syrian enamelled and gilded vase. Probably Damascus or Aleppo. About 1325

24 Syrian enamelled mosque lamp. Damascus or Aleppo. About 1350

25 Syrian enamelled vase. Damascus or Aleppo. About 1375

26 Enamelled armorial dish. Venice. Early 16th century or possibly late 15th century

27 *Latticinio (Vitro di trina)* glass dish. Venice. Late 16th century

28 Enamelled goblet. Venice. About 1525

29 Winged drinking glass. Venice. Late 16th or early 17th century

30 A slightly later glass than 29, the central stem disappearing. 17th century

31 *Latticinio* vase or ewer with vermicular collar. Venice. 16th century

32 Vase or possibly *Humpen*. German *façon de Venise*. 16th century

33 *Humpen*, enamelled with serial pictures of the cooper's art

34 *Guttrolf* or *Angster*. German. Late 17th or early 18th century

35 *Passglas*. German. 16th century

36 Covered enamelled and gilt goblet. Bohemia or Silesia. 18th century

37 Engraved goblet with hunting scene. Germany (Nuremberg). *c.* 1665

38 Diamond engraved *Römer* of the Berkemeier type. Netherlands. 1600–25

39 and 40 Two *Römers* of typical proportions. Late 17th or early 18th century

41 Ice or crackle glass with mascarons and a bulbous mould-blown stem. 16th century

42 The adaptation of the Venetian style to the less flamboyant Northern taste. Late 16th century. Netherlands

43 and 44 The typical Dutch development of *Façon de Venise*. Both mid-17th century

45 Cantir, from which the contents are poured into the mouth without physical contact. Spanish (Catalonia). 18th century

73   An early incised twist wine in soda-metal with a folded foot
74   A later and more refined version in lead-metal. The bowl
     is moulded and the foot plain
75   Multiple spiral air-twist with Vermicular collar at centre
     of stem. The twist continues into the base of the bowl
76   M.S.A.T. with domed foot and engraved bowl. The com-
     bination is unusual
77   An ale-glass engraved with hops and barley. M.S.A.T.
     Folded foot
78   Corkscrew Mercury-twist. 1760–70
79   M.S.A.T. bucket bowl wheel-engraved with vine motif.
     Domed foot
80   Corkscrew cable of spirals. Saucer-top, round funnel
     bowl. Plain foot
81   M.S.A.T. entering base of bowl. Swelling knop. Plain foot
82   M.S.A.T. Two swelling knops. Folded foot
83   M.S.A.T. Shoulder knop and more angular central knop.
     Plain foot
84   M.S.A.T. Four simple knops causing loss of control of the
     twist. Domed foot
85   Multiple spiral opaque twist with saucer-top round funnel
     bowl and folded foot
86   Double series opaque twist with flute-moulded ogee bowl
     and plain foot
87   Ratafia glass. Double series opaque twist. Wheel-engraved
     bowl and plain foot
88   Double series opaque twist, the inner being a lace twist.
     Plain foot
89   Waisted ogee bowl. Double series opaque twist. Plain foot
90   Pan-topped, round-funnel bowl. The lower part being
     slightly fluted and wrythen. Plain foot
91   Norwich or Lynn bowl, here in conjunction with a folded foot
92   Waisted bucket bowl
93   A Dram with ogee bowl and terraced foot
94   Ogee bowl and domed foot
95   Ogee bowl. Plain foot and knop at centre of stem enclosing
     Maundy coin of 1754
96   Ogee bowl enamelled in white vine motif. Attributed to
     the Beilby family

Text Figures

Acknowledgements

THIS volume could not have been produced without the considerable assistance afforded by those to whom acknowledgement is made in relation to the illustrations and by the many firms, museums, libraries and private collectors both at home and abroad who have generously made available their collections and the fruits of their research. In particular I am indebted to the late W. A. Thorpe who gave invaluable help when the book was first conceived and suggested specialists who gave advice on the various subjects, to Miss Anthea Marshall who executed the drawings and to Miss Joan Hopwood who translated an illegible scrawl into an orderly typescript.

Prestbury, Cheshire   O. N. W.

Acknowledgement for kind permission to reproduce illustrations is made to the following bodies, to whom copyright of the illustrations belongs:

The Victoria and Albert Museum, London (Crown Copyright)
6, 7, 17, 18, 19, 20, 21, 25, 26, 27, 29, 30, 31, 32, 33, 34, 35, 39, 40, 41, 42, 43, 44, 69, 117, 119, 120, 121
The Royal Scottish Museum, Edinburgh
9, 10, 11, 12, 13, 14, 15, 16, 24, 51, 52, 53, 54, 55, 56, 70, 110, 111, 112, 113, 116
The Corning Museum of Glass, Corning
23, 28, 36, 37, 38, 45, 46, 49, 97, 122, 123, 124, 125
The Manchester City Art Galleries
71, 75, 76, 78, 81, 83, 84, 98, 99, 107, 109
The Trustees of the British Museum, London
8
The National Museum of Antiquities of Scotland, Edinburgh
22

The Science Museum, Kensington
4, 5
The Cecil Higgins Art Gallery, Bedford
50
The Royal Albert Museum, Exeter
47
Messrs. Delomosne & Son Ltd., London
48
Central Press Photos Ltd.
1, 2, 3
Birmingham City Museum and Art Gallery
118

Introduction

THE desire to collect antiques is all too often stifled by the fear that mistakes will be both inevitable and expensive. It is true that they are inevitable, but the expensive mistakes are made almost entirely by the collector who tries to run before he can walk. Many branches of antique-collecting involve a great deal of expenditure, but the collector of drinking glasses can still build up an interesting and representative collection with a minimum outlay. Some glasses cost thousands of pounds, some cost thirty or forty shillings; in the illustrations to this book are glasses in both categories, for a conscious effort has been made to include the sort of pieces which the beginner can expect to acquire without risk as well as the pieces which will for some time remain of purely academic interest.

There are on the market a great many books on glass, and the present volume is not intended to replace any one of these, nor does it pretend to be a textbook. The object throughout has been to supplement the standard books with the guidance which may help the beginner and which in so many books is considered unnecessary. Thus the reader must not expect a full picture of the manufacture and history of glass, but he may find certain aspects all too frequently omitted. No single writer is competent to review authoritatively an art which has developed internationally for nearly five thousand years, and all must choose limits. The limits chosen here are those which surround a study of eighteenth-century English drinking glasses, and accordingly the international history omits all mention of stained glass, chandeliers, and the myriad uses to which glass has been put. An appetite for knowledge will not be satisfied, but it is to be hoped that it will be whetted. If the reader avoids one expensive mistake, then this book will have served its purpose.

The written word will in all probability be the source of most of the beginner's knowledge, but he must read with an open mind, for he will find considerable disagreement between authors. This volume is at variance with many of the established

15

authorities; but the continual acceptance of certain facts restricts research and the sacred cows are often better slaughtered. Although every author strives for accuracy, error can easily creep in through misconstruction of a source or theory, and what is written here must be viewed in the light cast by other writers, and also in the light of the reader's own experience.

Basically this book is divided into three parts: a short description of those aspects of manufacture which are particularly relevant to the collector, a survey of the international development, and a rather more detailed study of English eighteenth-century glass. On each of these aspects the reader will find specialist books, and the present volume is intended as a supplemental guide, which may assist in the identification of a given piece, first by showing national and manufacturing characteristics, and then, if the glass is English, by circumscribing the possible date. It cannot act as a substitute for a prolonged visit to a glasshouse or for studying the more detailed works on the subject, to some of which reference is made either at the conclusion of each chapter or in the Bibliography that appears at the end.

The result of adopting this approach is necessarily an unbalanced picture of the history of glass. Certain of the omitted subjects are fields in which the reader should turn straight to the specialist books; other omissions occur because general information could mislead. This policy has been continued in the illustrations.

Glass has played an important part in civilisation, which is frequently overlooked. Without window-glass and lenses the life we lead would be very different, and while the reader is primarily concerned with the art forms of glass, he must remember that these represent only the playthings of civilisation and materially rank among the less valuable contributions that glass has made to man's life.

CHAPTER ONE

The Art of Glassmaking

ANY work of art may be appreciated in two ways. One may look at it and see only the aesthetic qualities of the finished work or one may look at it analytically and observe the difficulties overcome by its creator. The collector of old glass may obtain much pleasure without any knowledge of its manufacture, yet even the slightest acquaintance with the problems will enhance that pleasure a thousandfold. To study every facet of manufacturing technique would probably confuse the collector rather than help him, but there are certain facets which deserve his attention, not necessarily because they are important stages of glassmaking, but because they may provide the answer to his queries. Why does some clear glass have a green tint? Why are there bubbles in this piece? Why is that piece lop-sided? What causes brown marks on a glass? Why is the underside of old wineglasses rough?

In this chapter attention is paid more to answering such questions as these than to providing a complete picture of glassmaking. In order to obtain such a picture the reader must visit a glasshouse, for he will learn more there in an hour than any book can teach him in a week. It is enough here to dwell on the problems that most concern the collector.

Perhaps the best-known description of glassmaking is the story told by Pliny of the discovery of glass. The story is undoubtedly apocryphal, but, like so many apocryphal stories, there is enough truth and possibility to command attention and justify repetition.

Pliny lived in the first century A.D., by which time glassmaking was a well-established industry, and from other passages in his work it is clear that he had more than a superficial knowledge of how the metal was made; the story that follows is therefore not such as one would expect him to tell, unless he believed it to be true.

Some Phoenician merchants, says Pliny, travelling between Egypt and Syria, landed one night on the shores of the estuary of the River Belus and lit their camp fire. Their cargo being blocks of natron (a form of soda), they used these to support their cooking pots and in the morning discovered that the natron and sand had fused to form glass.

The story has both its bad and its good points. The sand in the estuary of the Belus is suitable for making glass, and natron is a perfectly reasonable flux. Indeed, silica sand can be induced to form a glass-like substance without any flux; this necessitates an extremely high temperature, but the resultant metal is extremely strong. Natron would lower considerably the temperature required, and it is just possible that the camp fire could sustain the heat long enough to create at least partial fusion. However, the metal described by Pliny is soluble in water (the solution is known to us as water-glass and is used as a preservative and in the manufacture of adhesives), so some stabiliser is essential to create a durable metal. The commonest is lime and this appears to have been the stabiliser used in the earliest glass about 3000 B.C.

We should therefore not wholly discard Pliny's version, but view it in the light shed for us by a knowledge of the technique of manufacture and an appreciation of what constitutes glass.

Turning first to the technique of manufacture, one point in Pliny's story immediately invites comment. The process of making iron may be regarded in some measure as an allied art, and one cannot rule out the possibility that glass was discovered not accidentally, but as the result of research by those making iron. This may, however, have been research based on the chance discovery detailed by Pliny. It is, none the less, a long step from the unstable silica-soda fusion to the stable silica-soda-lime metal. The constitution of even the earliest known stable metal suggests that it resulted from extensive experiments and, the iron industry having advanced rapidly, it is probable that the early ironmakers wondered just how much of the earth beneath them could be melted. To attempt to melt sand appears a logical step after melting iron ore. The three essential ingredients of this metal known as 'soda-glass' are silica, soda, and lime. They are mixed roughly in the proportion 60:25:15, although the margin of error is considerable.

The greatest failing of soda metal was that it lacked the appearance of natural crystal. This appearance has always represented the ultimate goal of the glassmaker, for natural crystal has no ductility and must be carved. The limitations thus imposed made an artificial form that could be shaped at will appear highly desirable. Throughout the history of glassmaking we shall see that there are periods of intensive research to find the perfect metal, but it was not until the seventeenth century that the quest reached a decisive point. Then, almost simultaneously, two solutions were reached. In Bohemia it was discovered that a fusion of silica, potash, and lime produced a metal of greater lustre and crystal-like nature, and in England George Ravenscroft made the technical break-through which gave us the earliest form of that deep-lustred, crystal-clear metal known as lead- or flint-glass. This latter metal, which is and always has been more expensive to produce than soda metal, approaches most nearly the ultimate goal.

Again the basis is silica – although it has been suggested without authentication that the term 'flint' arises from the fact that Ravenscroft used ground flint instead – to which are added red lead and potash so that the proportions of the metal are 45:30:25. Again, as with soda metal, there is a wide tolerance, and the extensive range of lead-glass metals gives some indication of the infinite varieties of silica and the other basic ingredients used in varying proportions.

The silica necessary for glassmaking is generally taken from inland sources of sand – rather than the sea-shore – and in this respect England is exceptionally fortunate. Not only are there sufficient sources to satisfy the country's requirements, but also enough to cater for a thriving export business, which may appear strange when so much is imported from Fontainebleau and also the Netherlands. It may seem unreasonable that the sand round England's shores should be spurned, but the advantages of inland sand are considerable. First of all, the sand can be ground down to a regularity of grain unattainable from sea sand, a fact which in turn leads to better fusion. Secondly, there is far less obvious foreign matter to be removed; and thirdly, the concealed impurities are less frequent. Of these impurities the great enemy of the glassmaker is undoubtedly iron, for iron oxide, even if forming only an infinitesimal fraction of the total ingredients of a 'batch' of glass, can impart a distinctly green tint to the finished metal. One part in ten thousand will make

a difference and the extra effort involved in entirely removing
the impurity accounts for the fact that a great deal of industrial
glass is green. Since the only effect is on the colour, in most
cases the detriment is minimal. Obviously the impurities must
be removed if the object is to produce a clear metal, and this is
achieved by washing, heating, and sieving. The treatment today
is a highly scientific process, and yet even so certain impurities
have to be neutralised chemically; the purity of the natural
deposit was in a less scientific era than our own of paramount
importance. The countering of remaining impurities is considered later in this chapter.

The soda element of the metal is derived from common salt
by carbonation. Potash, which is generally preferred where
economy is not of prime importance, was formerly obtained by
extracting the salts from wood ash in solution and subsequent
evaporation. This, however, creates the usual hazard of impurities, and now potassium chloride in its chemical form has to
a great extent replaced the more tedious process of derivation.

In England there are also deposits of limestone relatively free
from impurity, and the siting of early glasshouses may occasionally be governed by local availability of silica and lime, provided always that there is adequate fuel for the furnaces in the
area.

Lead is employed in the form of red lead, which ideally is
90 per cent lead and 10 per cent free oxygen. A more elementary
form of the oxide, known as litharge, was used initially, but this
presented considerable problems to the makers in that, unless
maintained in its oxidised form, its metallic nature tended to
colour the glass. In the dioxide form this problem becomes of
minor importance.

In setting out as above the basic ingredients of the metal,
there may have been a tendency to oversimplify. Other ingredients abound in even the most primitive examples known to us.
Borax, originally used for its value as a flux, is also employed
to give the metal greater resistance to chipping; arsenic, which
has a beautifying effect in many fields, has been employed for
centuries to add brilliance to the metal; oxide of tin can be used
to give the metal an opaque nature, and innumerable additives
give it varying colours. Some of the principal colouring agents
are set out below; they will produce varying results, dependent

on the other constituents of the metal and their own state of oxidisation.

Iron	Green, blue, and yellow
Cobalt	Blue
Gold	Ruby red
Copper	Green, blue, and red
Iron and Copper	Black
Nickel	Violet (in lead-glass)

The list of colouring agents could be extended indefinitely, these agents often occurring as impurities in one or other of the main components. The process of countering unwanted colour was known to the Roman glassmakers, and they achieved considerable success on occasion; but it is doubtful whether they ever reduced it to a science such as it is today.

Perhaps the easiest way to envisage the countering process is to imagine the light spectrum as a pair of scales. If iron is present in the metal, the light transmission at one end of the spectrum is impaired and, while the transmission cannot be improved again, the colour can be eliminated by balancing the spectrum with manganese oxide, which affects the other end of the colour scale. The more balancing that takes place the less light is transmitted, until ultimately one has a metal that is virtually black. For example, overcorrection of the balance can result in a green tint giving way to a mauve tint, caused by the overbalancing effect of manganese oxide. The less balancing necessary, the better the refraction of light and the more brilliant the metal – hence the importance of the initial purity of the ingredients.

Having observed briefly the constituent parts of the batch, we can now turn to the manufacture of the basic metal. The maker, having selected his materials with such care in order to avoid impurity, exercises similar care to ensure that the pot in which fusion will take place is free from any substance with a deleterious effect on the contents.

The manufacture of a glass pot is itself a fascinating process, for it taxes the potter's skill. The larger the vessel, the greater the risk of a crack appearing during firing; the making of a pot about four feet high and three feet in diameter, or possibly larger, therefore presents considerable hazards.

Failure of the pot can prove extremely costly, not only because the contents are wasted – and in some cases the pot will contain nearly a ton – but also because the process of manufacture is a prolonged and exacting task. Additional cost is incurred in the treatment of the clay, which is subjected to purification processes not dissimilar to those used to purify the silica, before it reaches the potter.

The rate at which a pot can be built is governed to prevent any compression that might result in the development of flaws. In a vessel of this size and weight a too rapid building of the wall will inevitably cause a bulge, which invites subsequent disaster.

When the pot is complete it is permitted to dry out naturally, although the heat and moisture content of the drying chamber are carefully regulated. However, the firing itself is the supreme test; for, even if everything has gone well so far, the pot must now withstand temperatures far in excess of those it will sustain during its working life. Then, while still extremely hot, it is moved to the furnace, a movement fraught with danger, owing to the change of atmospheric temperatures. Only when it is safely installed can the maker relax, knowing that his pot will withstand the vicissitudes of the glasshouse for between ten and twenty weeks. Thereafter the pot will probably be replaced, since its reliability becomes suspect.

There are two common types of glass pot with which we are concerned (the use of tanks is relatively recent and not relevant to our subject), these being the open or 'skittle' pot, which resembles a long narrow barrel open at the top, and the 'crown' covered pot with a domed top and a small side opening which can be sealed.

The skittle pot is still occasionally used for soda-glass and coloured glass, the practice being more common abroad than in Britain. It is cheaper to produce, but its open top permits the surface of the metal to be exposed to impurities in the furnace. Until it was appreciated that this furnace contamination was one of the causes of colouring, the open pots were mainly bucket-shaped, as in Plates 4 and 5, with a far larger surface area.

The crown pot used for lead-glass can be stoppered during melting, thus restricting oxidisation and contamination of the contents. In the case of clear, colourless lead-glass this is vital, and the side opening allows for removal of a stopper without unnecessary fouling of the metal.

The design of the furnace to which the pot is taken has changed but little over the centuries. The means of heating the furnace has improved radically, but the general principle remains the same: a fire chamber below and the pot chamber above.

Examples of early furnaces, reconstructed from contemporary descriptions, are illustrated in Plates 4 and 5 and, in view of the minor changes over the last eight centuries, it is reasonable to suspect that many of the earlier furnaces, of which only the ruins have been discovered, were of much the same design.

We can now turn to the actual melting of the glass. The mixture, known as 'batch', is placed in the pot together with a quantity of broken glass, or 'cullet', which helps fusion; incidentally, this step also largely excludes wastage in the glasshouse.

The pot, stoppered if necessary, is then heated to high temperature (c. 1500°C). In this respect the modern furnaces, whether gas- or oil-fired, have great advantages; electricity is not widely used. Temperatures are more easily sustained, and the use of heat regeneration enables the modern manufacturer to avoid a fault extremely common in old glass. As the constituents fuse, bubbles of gas are created, and unless these are brought to the surface during melting they remain in the metal as 'seed'. This defect is found today only in the products of the smaller furnaces, since elimination presents no problems to the established makers with modern furnaces. Before elimination by high temperatures was possible the makers had to resort to the process of partial fusion, followed by the grinding of the resultant mass and remelting. The presence of 'seed' in old glass is a reasonable indication that it has been produced in an inadequately heated furnace, and is a more common feature in metal of the period when wood was used as the main fuel.

Eventually the metal reaches a state in which it is completely fluid and extraordinarily brilliant. It is then permitted to cool until it reaches a treacly consistency at which the glassmaker can make a gathering, or 'paraison', on the end of his blowing-iron. The metal at this stage has remarkable ductile qualities which are best illustrated in the manufacture of glass cane. If a gathering is given a triangular cross-section, it will retain that cross-sectional shape however much it is drawn out lengthwise.

Since this book deals primarily with tableware, the process of shaping the finished article is best described in following the stages of manufacture of a simple wineglass. The basic principle, however, remains the same in all glass-blowing.

The manufacture of any blown-glass product is a study in teamwork; time is an important factor and it is impractical for one man to perform all the operations. The making of a wine-glass is the work of a gang or 'chair', consisting of three men headed by the 'gaffer', and usually a number of apprentices.

Sufficient glass is first gathered on the blowing-iron, a hollow rod generally about 4 feet in length, by dipping it in the pot and revolving it on the surface of the molten metal. The gather-ing is then 'marvered', or rolled on a slab of iron (marble in the very early days of glass), in order to compact it and eliminate irregularities and bubbles which may form in the gathering. The blower then blows enough air to create a small balloon (see Plate 2). To the other end of this is added the glass for the stem, which will have been prepared by another member of the chair, or alternatively the end of the balloon may be drawn out to form a stem. The blowing-iron is now at what will ultimately be the top of the finished glass. A small bubble of glass is gathered for the foot on another iron, and when attached (see Plate 1) to the stem is either shaped from a solid piece or, if the foot is blown, cut open with shears and shaped, the edges occasionally being turned in to form what is known as a 'folded foot'. Most wineglasses are of either two- or three-piece construction (i.e. bowl-stem and foot, or bowl, stem, and foot), although in some cases the stem may itself be built up of two or three pieces.

The cup part of the glass is still in the shape of a balloon attached to the blowing-iron. In order to finish this end of the glass, a solid iron rod or 'pontil' is attached to the exact centre of the foot, and the top half of the cup-balloon is then removed by 'wetting-off' (applying a wet iron) where the rim is to be. The surplus is then sheared off and the gaffer can finish the glass (see Plate 3).

Before dealing with the finishing of the glass, we must retrace our steps a little to see just how much shape is induced in the actual blowing. At this stage the glass, being soft, is still liable to collapse under its own weight, and the workman uses gravity, centrifugal force, and blowing to avoid collapse and to achieve the shape he desires. In order to do this he may use the chair, which is basically a seat with long parallel arms sloping slightly away from him. This he uses as a lathe, and the glass is kept revolving as the rod is rolled back and forth along the arms of the chair with the palm of the left hand, leaving the right hand free to work on the glass.

The balloon may be blown into a ribbed mould and the ribs subsequently drawn together to form a trellis pattern, known for the last two or three centuries as 'nipt diamond-waies' (generally abbreviated to N.D.W.), and then blown a little more to make the pattern less harsh. Once the stem and foot are attached, the pontil is fixed on with a small blob of molten glass. The 'gadget' (or spring pontil), which is a sort of spring clip on the end of a rod, tended to replace the pontil after about 1800 for certain types of work (e.g. heavy pieces), thus obviating the necessity of having an extra blob of glass to fix the pontil, which has eventually to be removed. For normal pieces the ordinary pontil continues in use today. No authoritative evidence can be found to support the contention that the gadget was in use at all prior to 1760, although certain marks on the feet of earlier glasses are often attributed to this tool.

The gaffer, having separated the blowing-iron, is now left with a recognisable wineglass, mounted the correct way up on the pontil or gadget. The bowl must now be opened out to the desired shape, and this he does by rolling the pontil across the chair and shaping the bowl with 'pucellas', which resemble tongs. Originally these were made entirely of metal, and on old glass it is not uncommon to find iron-marks left by the pucellas. Eventually it was found that wooden ends gave a better finish and iron-marks are unusual after about 1750. (Some of the gaffer's tools are to be seen in Plate 2 and the gadget or spring pontil in Plate 3.)

During the processes outlined above, it is probable that the glass will have been returned to the 'glory-hole', or mouth of a subsidiary furnace, to maintain it in its ductile state, to soften the sharp edges and also to restore the fire polish.

Once the glass has been finished it is removed to the warm annealing chamber, which will allow it to cool gradually. This is a most important process, since during the shaping various stresses will have been set up in the metal, and, if it were allowed to cool quickly, not only would these stresses affect the durability of the glass, but also the more rapid cooling of the outer layers of the metal would set up fresh irregular stresses. The wineglass shattered by the voice of a singer is more a criticism of the way the glass has been annealed than a tribute to the voice; any vibrant sound will achieve the same result, because the vibration set up in the glass is absorbed irregularly and fracture follows. Similarly, glass which chips easily is often the result of bad annealing, although it can also represent a lack of borax or a badly constituted batch.

The decorative processes applied to glass fall into two categories: those applied during the actual making of the object and those applied after the basic manufacture is completed.

Into the first category fall the moulded decorations and the superimposed trails and seals. Moulding is one of the oldest forms of ornamentation, yet one which has lent itself ideally to modern mass production. Press-moulding, which became popular in the nineteenth century with the advance of mechanisation, creates far less limitation on the shape of an object than the early two-piece mould, since sections may now be moulded separately and pressed together. Trailed decoration and seals of metal (known as 'prunts' and often impressed with a pattern) are also the discovery of the early makers, who used them as relief upon the plain vessel. While these forms have endured throughout the history of glass, they are recurrent rather than consistent.

From the point of view of the collector the most interesting forms in this category are probably the introduction of bubbles or 'tears' and the clear- and opaque-twists found in wineglass stems.

Tears are obtained by 'pegging' – the insertion of a tool into the hot glass – which leaves a hollow. When the pegging hole is covered with hot glass the air is imprisoned; gravity and the heat expansion of the trapped air then decide the shape of the tear. Since the glass is still slightly liable to collapse at this stage, the shape of the tear will indicate just what risks the maker has taken; if he is to avoid collapse it may be necessary to hold the glass one way up while, to attain a certain shape of tear, he may wish to hold it the other way. 'Prince Rupert's drops', the little hollow tear-shaped glass baubles once used by ladies of fashion like sequins, were occasionally introduced instead, but the process was not satisfactory and examples, though rare, are clumsy.

The making of the clear air-twists (in certain forms called mercury-twists because of the visual effect, see Plates 75–84) calls for considerable skill. The metal is introduced into a cylindrical mould of which the interior face is grooved perpendicularly. When the moulded metal is removed it is coated with hot glass and the ends sealed, leaving a series of long tubes of air trapped. The glass is then drawn out until the requisite thickness for the stem is achieved, the air tubes becoming thinner in the process; a strip is then taken off and twisted to form spirals. The complexity of this operation renders a twist within a twist an uncommon feature and a considerable feat of craftsmanship. The air-twist may also be achieved by pegging the paraison and then stretching and twisting it; but this process has not acquired the popularity of the moulded method, since it involves not only greater skill but also creates a less regular twist.

Opaque-twists (see Plates 85–99) present rather less difficulty in manufacture. A number of opaque glass canes are set in the grooves of the mould and the same process repeated as in the moulded form of air-twist, but since one is here dealing with a solid mass it is much easier to manipulate and create compound twists. The creation of *millefiori* glass, originating from principles similar to those of the manufacture of the opaque-twist, will be discussed in the chapter on Venetian glass.

The introduction of gold leaf between two layers of glass has been known from a very early date, but since the gold leaf tended to be distorted from its original design the practice has not found general favour.

After the glass has passed from the hands of the glassblower it can receive additional decoration by gilding, enamelling, cutting, and engraving.

Gilding can be achieved in either of two ways. The design may be varnished into the glass and gold leaf set on top so that when the varnish dries out the gold leaf adheres to the body of the glass. This method does not create an enduring effect, but has been used extensively to colour engraved portions of a glass. Many old engraved glasses will be found to have minimal traces of the old gilt. The other method, which is more enduring, is to mix the gilt in powder form with a flux and then to paint it on to the metal, using an oil medium. The glass is then heated to a point where the fluxed gilt will fuse without melting the main body of the glass.

Enamelling embodies the same principles, but here colouring agents take the place of the gold leaf. Again the question of durability is to be considered, a great deal of nineteenth-century glass having already lost its enamelling owing to the popularity at that time of the less enduring method. Where the enamel is applied with flux there is always the danger of shrinkage and distortion, but this varies according to the type of flux used; borax is generally considered to be the most reliable.

Glass cutting, one of the oldest processes and one of the most consistently popular, achieved its climax with the advent of lead-glass, which retains its brilliance even when it has the thickness necessary for cutting and is less liable to chip on the wheel. The object to be cut is held to the abrasive wheel rather than vice versa and is finished by using less abrasive polishing wheels. The quality of the cutting depends entirely on the freehand skill of the workman; for the depth and direction of any cut once started cannot be annealed without the alternative being apparent in the refraction of the finished work. The forms and limitations of this art will be discussed later.

Engraving takes three principal forms, the most widely used being wheel engraving. Here a small copper wheel, kept moist with an abrasive feed, is rotated at high speed to dull the surface of the glass, seldom cutting into the metal as much as $\frac{1}{32}$ inch. Diamond-point engraving takes two forms: the diamond or steel point is used either to scratch the surface or else to stipple it and build up a picture much as a newspaper photograph is made up by the varying frequency of the dots.

Finally there is etching; for glass, although resistant to most acids, is affected by hydrofluoric acid. The surface of the glass is covered with a varnish or wax 'resist' which is then cut away to bare the metal in accordance with the design. The acid is then allowed to react on the bare metal for a very short period before it is washed and the resist taken off.

Each of these decorative techniques has its own place in the history of glass and each will again be discussed in its chronological context. The present summary is intended only to outline the processes.

For further reference:

CHARLESTON, R. J. 'Lead in Glass', *Archaeometry*.

DOUGLAS, R. W. 'Glass Technology', *A History of Technology*, ed. Singer, Vol. V, pp. 671–82.

ELVILLE, E. M. *English Table Glass*.

HUMPHREY, M. C. 'The Atomic Structure of Glass and its Consequences', *Transactions of the Circle of Glass Collectors*, No. 120.

KING, J. 'Lead in Glass and Glaze', *Museums Journal*, Vol. 56, No. 12, pp. 281–4.

TURNER, W. E. S. Various articles in *Transactions of the Society of Glass Technology*.

CHAPTER TWO

The Early Development of Glass

THE early history of glass is almost entirely theoretical, since the factual evidence is extremely limited. Every new archaeological discovery leads to a new theory, which may be accepted or rejected according to the weight of factual evidence supporting it and the degree of proof required by any particular researcher. The account which follows seeks to achieve a combination of those theories old or new which do not break the slender thread of continuity spun by the factual evidence, but the reader should not accept this or any other account without a measure of scepticism.

The place and date at which glass was first discovered are, despite Pliny's confident account, totally unknown, but it is safe to say that the date was prior to 3000 B.C. In the light of archaeological finds, speculation as to the place is now being confined to the areas of Syria, Egypt, and Mesopotamia. The principal reason for favouring these areas is that they abounded in the natural materials and in fuel; although we think today of Egypt as being fairly arid, the Nile valley was at one time very much wider and thickly wooded.

Glass in the form of a vitreous glaze was certainly known to the Egyptians before 3000 B.C., and the decorative techniques found on Egyptian pottery bear a distinct resemblance to the decoration of the earliest glass forms that we know. However, all the specimens we have from Egypt suggest that the art had long since passed the purely experimental stage.

One of the earliest pieces of evidence we have is a green bead discovered by Sir Flinders Petrie at Naqada. This measures less than ¼ inch across, but, from its location in the strata, can confidently be dated between 3000 and 2500 B.C. Petrie himself gave it the earlier date, but subsequent authorities have suggested that he was unduly optimistic. Its place of manufacture is uncertain; it may not even be Egyptian, since the earliest glass furnace found in Egypt is not very much earlier than the well-known remains at Tell el-Amarna, which date to about

1400 B.C. The earlier wall paintings at Beni Hasan were originally thought to show the process of glassmaking, although it is now generally accepted that these represent another metallic process; these date from the XIth Dynasty (c. 2000 B.C.), but they have never been accepted as satisfactory evidence of a glass industry in Egypt.

Factors in support of Syria as a claimant to the discovery are its geographical suitability, the story known to Pliny, and glass finds dating back to about 2500 B.C. It is certain that, when the Egyptians conquered Syria, Tahutmes III took back captive Syrian craftsmen, and the supporters of Syria suggest that the Egyptian industry was started in this manner.

Petrie described in some detail how the first glass vessels were made, and, although it is largely a matter of speculation, there is little reason to suspect that he was not close to the truth.

The process is known as 'core-winding'. Basically a ball of clay or sand is bound up and tied into a compact shape. Glass trails are then wound round the ball, which is held on a metal rod, and the whole is reheated periodically until the ball is completely and uniformly covered. Then by marvering the glass and superimposing the desired pattern the vessel is completed. After annealing, the metal rod is broken clear of the neck and the sand scraped out. This technique was undoubtedly used in the vessel shown in Plate 6.

The Egyptians reached a very high artistic standard by about 1000 B.C. and then for 300 or 400 years we have remarkably little evidence of the industry in Egypt, although quite clearly glassmaking continued in countries surrounding the Mediterranean.

When the industry did revive in Egypt, it revived in very much the same form as when it disappeared, although it has been suggested that Greek influences are apparent. In view of the paucity of Greek specimens prior to 600 B.C. and the marked similarity to earlier Egyptian glass, the effect of such an influence is probably overrated. In the meantime, it is true, other Mediterranean countries had advanced, but by 500 B.C. two predominant styles had begun to emerge: Egyptian and Syrian. Before discussing the development of these styles, however, we must consider just when the practice of blowing glass originated; for there is no evidence of a transitional stage from core-winding and the all too long accepted date of *c*. 50 B.C. is supported by very little substantial evidence. Recent discoveries at Gordion and elsewhere of what looks like blown glass of origin undoubtedly earlier than 50 B.C. are causing some fresh consideration of the problem. There is a way in which an amphora may be blown that will reproduce the characteristics of a core-wound vessel while differing little from modern blowing techniques.

Today, if one wished to blow an amphora, the normal practice would be to blow the body, finish the base, fix a pontil to it, and sever the blowing-iron and 'overblow' (i.e. the surplus metal) from the mouth. It is perfectly possible that the early makers blew the body and finished the mouth at the end away from the iron; then with a rod placed down the finished mouth, and adhering to it, they closed the foot at the blowing-iron end and cracked off the overblow. The process of annealing would certainly be simplified if the object were filled with sand to prevent a lop-sided collapse. This method eliminates the awkward question of how one obtains a core which will hold together, while threads are wound round it and exposed to fresh heat, and yet come out through a narrow neck on completion; some of the core-wound vessels have inconveniently narrow necks.

If this theory is accepted, despite the lack of evidence to support it, then the absence of an obvious transitional stage is not surprising and the date of the introduction of glass-blowing may be set within very wide limits.

The centuries prior to the Christian era represent a period in which the decorative techniques developed to a far greater extent than the composition of the metal. As early as the fourth century B.C. gold leaf appears as a form of decoration fired between two layers of glass, and in the third century moulded and sculptures glass makes its first appearance. This latter form, later to be known as *diatreta* (literally 'rubbed away'), is generally taken to mean glass on which the pattern stands clear of the body of the vessel, being held to it only by glass links; Fremersdorf limited its meaning to that glass in which a thick body was carved and undercut, a technique of which few examples exist. The word was later applied also to work where an overlay of a different colour was cut away to leave a cameo decoration, as, for example, in the Portland Vase; the use of the word in Latin authors often leaves obscure to which technique reference is made. In the first century B.C. the industry received a terrific impetus which may be attributed either to the discovery of glass-blowing or alternatively to the rapidly growing wealth of Rome.

The next four centuries are generally divided into the periods Roman I and II. The division is one of convenience, based on an arbitrary date of A.D. 200, rather than of distinction of style, and it is far safer and less confusing to divide the era by style into Syrian and Alexandrian. Rome itself was never a glass-making centre of any importance, and the term 'Roman' as applied to glass is something of a misnomer, although to the Romans must go the credit for establishing conditions in which the art could spread in the wake of their conquests. The makers of glass were, however, the Syrians, the Alexandrians, and their disciples.

Apart from the utility glass made by both schools for purely commercial reasons, the styles are reasonably distinct. The Syrian makers tend to exhibit a more flamboyant naturalistic style, blowing works of inspired shape and indulging in extravagant fancies. The metal in which they worked was light in weight, generally yellow or green and seldom colourless, and technically a poor material.

The Alexandrians, on the other hand, were somewhat pedestrian and formal in their styles; having mastered the material and produced a fine metal, their artistry is more a tribute to technique and detailed craftsmanship than to any inspiration. The imitation of marble was an Alexandrian achievement and this they turned to good purpose by reproducing in glass the stone 'murrines' or fancy goods which were so popular an export from Egypt (see Plate 10).

Cutting and engraving were precision arts in which the Alexandrian workmen excelled, and they perfected, if not discovered, the art of making the various forms of *diatreta*. One example of their skill in this field is the Portland or Barberini Vase.

The Vase is interesting from several points of view and justifies a slight digression from the main tenor of this chapter. As can be seen in Plate 8, the Vase is a two-handled vessel with the proportions of an amphora lacking the lower part – the true amphora shape can be seen in Plate 16. Measuring about 10 inches in height, it is made of blue metal with a white overlay carved away to leave the cameo decoration, which, in its turn, is ground to create light and shade. This effect is heightened by the blue beneath darkening the thinner opaque-white areas. The workmanship of the cameo, which surrounds the entire Vase and also appears on the base, is superb, and virtually defies reproduction today as a commercial proposition. We do not know whether it was made as a single specimen or if it is merely representative of a class of which no comparable examples have survived. Nor do we know whether it was produced on an economic basis or represented the fulfilment of an ideal regardless of cost.

Since it was manufactured, in the first or second century A.D., the Vase has had a chequered history, even though this is known in detail only from the mid-eighteenth century. At one time in the possession of Sir William Hamilton, the British Ambassador in Naples, the Vase ultimately entered the collection of the Duke of Portland, who lent it to the British Museum. In 1845, while on display, it was shattered by a young Welshman and is now skilfully restored.

There remains, however, something of a mystery concerning the Vase, since it is doubtful whether the present shape is the original one. The late W. A. Thorpe, whose expertise in the field of glass is universally acknowledged, unfortunately never set out at length the grounds for his personal belief that the Vase was not in its original form; the views set out here are not necessarily in accordance with those of Thorpe, although it is probable that the same lines of approach have appealed both to Thorpe and the present writer.

First let us consider the present shape of the Vase; few will admit that it is beautiful. The over-all impression must be of a rather squat, stunted amphora sawn off some distance above its natural base. The shape is not typically Alexandrian and, were it not for the relief-work, would excite little interest. It is hard to believe that a craftsman with such an appreciation of the beautiful would prefer to execute his cameo on this shape rather than the true amphora, which would almost certainly have been available to him. The argument that the Vase has stability to commend it has no validity, for the base is covered with cameo work which would not be seen.

The cameo work ceases at the level of the handles, allowing the plain blue metal above to set off the cameo to advantage; below there is nothing. This not only distracts attention from the intricate work in the lower part of the cameo but also exposes it to the knocks inevitably sustained at the foot of any vessel. A lower plain section would both enhance and preserve.

The present base of the Vase is almost certainly not the original, differing as it does in colour and texture from the rest of the overlay. If the Vase was originally a stable vessel, why introduce a cameo which renders the stability of the vessel undesirable? If, however, it was unstable before, stability would be of limited importance in the restoration.

It is not unduly difficult to surmise what may have happened. The tapered end of an amphora is particularly vulnerable, both because of its structure and its physical instability. If the tapered end was broken, the piece is not such that the owner would willingly dispose of it, and in the circumstances the repairs were both sensible and well executed. It is unknown when this occurred, if indeed the basic theory is right, since the documentation we have covers so small a fraction of the Vase's life.

Speculation as to the shape of the Vase should not, however, blind us to the magnificence of the cameo.

We have so far considered only the art forms of glass, but both Syrian and Alexandrian workmen produced window-glass, glass mosaics – of which the popularity in Rome was such that they were even used, somewhat impractically, as flooring in their baths – and bottles. This last field produced two shapes of note, the Syrian tall round bottle, similar to a modern Chianti bottle, and the so-called Roman square, an angular bottle which was almost certainly of Alexandrian origin and far more suited to the conditions of travel of the day. The development of the bottle can be seen in Plates 17, 18, and 19. In certain spheres the distinction between the two styles becomes obscure, but the Syrian styles spread more quickly than the Alexandrian.

Throughout the history of glass national styles are confused by the fact that Syrian workmen were inclined to travel from place to place, according to the political climate and the demand for their wares, to a far greater extent than the Alexandrians. This is in some measure reflected in the limited periods during which certain manufacturing centres have thrived. Few arts have a history in which mobility of craftsmen plays such an important part as the art of glassmaking.

Under the peaceful conditions established by the Romans the industry flourished and spread northwards in the wake of the conquests, both in the form of exports and the initiation of local production. With the dual processes of blowing and moulding in use, there have been found innumerable examples of glass dating from the first to fourth centuries, and there is undoubtedly much which remains to be brought to light.

By A.D. 300, however, the Empire was no longer the compact unit it had been, and at about this time the capital was moved to Byzantium. Also Christianity was adopted as the State religion, which, from the archaeologist's point of view, was disastrous. Most of the specimens we have from the first four centuries of the Christian era owe their preservation to the enduring pagan custom of providing the dead with such possessions as were deemed essential to a full enjoyment of life in the next world. With the lapse of this custom in southern Europe, our knowledge of glass in the area becomes restricted to the few Christian glasses that have survived, so it is desirable to seek the continuing links in countries where there is more evidence. Although the political climate in Italy became progressively less conducive to the creation of works of art, it must not be supposed that no glass was made in Italy after the fourth century. Doubtless there was, but the pieces can have had little to distinguish them from the products of other countries.

The move to Byzantium was a logical one for Constantine to make; Rome was threatened by the barbarous hordes in the north and the wealth of Rome had come primarily from the east. One of the results of this move was to open up the way to fresh eastern influences, and we find the Romano-Syrian styles and the styles of the north-east Mediterranean merging to produce a rich variety of glass, varying from the crude but tough Arabic of the sixth and seventh centuries to the richly enamelled Islamic mosque lamps of the fourteenth century.

Meanwhile, in Europe, the history of glassmaking becomes closely bound up with the rapidly changing political scene. The Roman Empire, having reached the peak of military achievement in the first and second centuries, was now faced with the difficult task of maintaining extensive boundaries against the depredation of the barbarous northern tribes – a task in no way simplified by the fact that certain parts of the Empire had minimal contact with Rome or Byzantium. Citizenship could be bought, and the militant blood of Rome had been watered down to such an extent that the Empire was inclined to rest on its laurels and enjoy the prosperity gained by its conquests, with little thought for the future. Inevitably, therefore, when the pagan Teutonic tribes of the north saw the wealth of their neighbours to the south and realised that their own expansion need not as hitherto be restricted to an easterly direction, there was little in the way of organised defence forces to prevent them turning south and west.

Undoubtedly the most serious threat was that of Attila and the trans-Caspian Huns. They found little resistance as they drove south until the numbers of the Goths and other tribes, whose relationship with Rome had at least been one of tolerant coexistence, were driven before them to a point where they formed a solid wall of resistance. Although Attila himself was a highly educated man and had lived the life of a well-to-do Roman while a hostage for an errant relative, the Huns as a race were totally destructive, having no culture of their own and scant regard for that of others. Their ultimate defeat therefore prevented a possible hiatus in the progress of civilisation.

It was not only the Huns, however, who viewed the un-defended boundaries with satisfaction; throughout the fourth and fifth centuries the northern borders of the Empire were subject to constant incursions, with the inevitable consequences for trade and culture; some of the invaders, such as the Lombards, penetrated far south into Italy without meeting any properly organised resistance.

In such circumstances it is scarcely surprising that an art such as glassmaking, dependent as it was on a race noted for its peripatetic inclinations, should suffer a serious decline in the south. The security and political stability which the glassmakers sought was only to be found in the isolated areas where more reliance was placed on local strength than on Rome. Aquileia, which had for so long been the commercial centre of the Adriatic, was sacked in A.D. 450, and it has been suggested that Venice provided a haven for its refugees. There is a growing body of evidence to suggest that Aquileia was also a glassmaking centre and that the art was introduced to Venice by these refugees.

The decay of the Roman Empire was a gradual process, building up to its climax in the fourth and fifth centuries, so in order to appreciate the far-reaching effects one must compare the compact unit of the Empire in about A.D. 200 with the unwieldy, ill-defended, and ill-defined territories which comprised the Empire in about 450–500.

Byzantium, although the centre of Roman wealth and the commercial link between east and west, was far from being the ideal administrative centre of the Empire. The wholesale incursions of the northern tribes into Italy disrupted administration of the western territories and the desultory warfare did little to encourage the production of works of art.

Accordingly if one is to follow the thread of glassmaking one must look now to the east, where Roman and Greek culture met Syrian, or to the north, where the Franks had established an empire with some degree of stability and where Christianity had not so strong a hold that the custom of burying grave goods had died out. Italy, as we have noted above, doubtless produced glass, but no distinctive characteristics emerge and it is probable that much of the production was of utility glass, for there is little evidence of luxury goods to support the existence of any thriving industry.

We have already seen that the glassmakers had fled to areas where there was some security and a civilised market. Among the places to which they may have gone is Aquileia, but the evidence to support this theory cannot be regarded as conclusive. If there was sufficient acceptable evidence, it would provide the vital link between Roman glass and that of Venice, a link which must at the moment be a matter of speculation. Certainly the Frankish centres attracted them, and it is possible that the Normandy glass industry was started by refugees at about this time.

The greatest centre of glassmaking in the period of the dissolution of the Western Empire is undoubtedly the area now commonly designated 'Seine-Rhine' from the rivers that form the rough boundaries of the area. The tastes of these northern races differed considerably from those of the south; as early as the third century we find a heavier and more sombre style of glass emerging in the north. Under Roman auspices this glass was widely exported, but, as Roman maritime protection faded out and the Roman road system fell into disrepair, exports became fewer and the makers began to concentrate on the requirements of the wealthy in the area surrounding their glasshouses. Thus, although early Seine-Rhine glass is found all over Europe, as time goes on there is less to be found in areas other than that of manufacture. Scandinavia and Britain were virtually cut off by A.D. 500 from imported glass, but there is little doubt that at least some indigenous production, however limited, continued for a while.

The style of glass from the Seine-Rhine area relates very much more to the Syrian than to the Alexandrian style, which is only adopted occasionally and even then in a much modified form. Western glass as a whole owes more to the Syrians, probably because the Alexandrian makers were not by nature so restless nor perhaps so concerned with the accumulation of wealth. A study of early Egyptian glassmaking invariably leaves one horrified at the scant regard paid to economic aspects; glasshouses were habitually set up in wildly impractical areas where one material abounded and all others presented tremendous transport problems. The Syrians, on the other hand, were essentially business-like.

Although the Syrian style prevailed in the Seine-Rhine area, it rapidly lost its major characteristics and developed the minor. The thin bulges, so typical of early Syrian glass, became much heavier to provide a firm base for the ornamentation which is the distinctive feature of Seine-Rhine glass, and blowing can for the next few centuries be regarded as of secondary importance to decoration, a status it was to retain until the Venetian glassmakers brought it back to the fore in the fifteenth and sixteenth centuries. The period we are now entering is one typified by trailed decoration and tooling.

The age did, however, produce some interesting and distinctive shapes; first and foremost of these is the beaker. The development of this shape follows a clear and remarkably simple line from the second century to the seventh. The early drinking bowl (or palm-cup as it was called from the only practical method of holding it), although it exists in its original shape throughout the period, is later seen in a form similar to a modern tumbler, from which it developed into a tall cylinder and thence to the conical shape where it finally lost its stability (see Plate 20). A few glasses of the later period have a rudimentary foot, but most are unstable, a fact which does not, as is suggested by some, imply that glasses were invariably drained at one draught, but rather that there were servants to hold the glass. There may even have been stands for these beakers, but none have come down to us.

The decoration of glass during this period is extremely varied. The basic glass is often mould-blown, and mixed colour begins to play a major part in decoration. Glass of the murrine type, or clear glass with blobs of colour marvered into the surface, is relatively frequent, but the basic metal is generally brown, yellow, or green in appearance, the last being most common. Coloured trailing, marvered into the surface, reappears for a short period, occasionally being feathered in the Alexandrian style.

Primarily, however, decoration is superimposed, and in the case of the beaker the most noteworthy form is the 'claw' (see Plate 21). This is not a particularly early development, and it is a feature confined to northern glass.

The claw probably originated as a blob on the side of the glass which so fell out of shape that it formed a claw-like projection, broad at the top and narrow where the peak of the blob fell back against the glass lower down. Eventually the claw was made to stand clear of the body of the glass like a rather clumsy handle; it could be either solid or blown. The method of manufacturing the blown form is as follows. When the body of the glass has been blown it is allowed to cool until it just resists inflation and then a blob of hot metal is placed where the top of the claw will be. The blob melts the side of the vessel at this point back to inflation heat and the blower resumes work until the claw is hollow. The lower end is then fastened to the glass. The process is repeated until the total effect is that of a number of ineffective loops handles fixed to the beaker, generally in either two or three tiers; glasses having only one tier are very much rarer. The style reached its acme about the end of the fifth century, by which time the beaker had changed back in shape from the tall cone to a rather more squat and certainly more solid vessel than it had been in the previous century. The earlier decoration of the beaker was very much in line with the forms found on other glass objects of the period, which we must now consider.

We have already noted that the thin, Syrian, blown bulge was going out of fashion in Europe and more solid mould-blown glass was taking its place. Horizontal and vertical ribbing and fluting, created by blowing into a mould, became a major feature of Seine-Rhine glass by the third century, and the glass was sometimes twisted to create a 'wrythen' effect. Alternatively, the ribbing might be tooled while the glass was still hot, two adjacent ribs being drawn together to create the diamond effect which is now known as 'nipt diamond-waies', a term first applied by Ravenscroft in the seventeenth century to this form of decoration.

From ribbing imposed in the mould it was but a short step to superimposed ribbing or trailing. This form can reasonably be divided into two classes: applied, as by means of a lathe (see Plates 20 and 21), and free-style. The method of using the former type of trailing is for the servitor to feed a thread of hot glass on to the object to be decorated as the gaffer turns it either on the chair or, more probably, across his knees, for at this period the available evidence suggests that the chair was not yet a normal feature of the glasshouse. Free-style trailing is applied much as one might apply icing decoration to a cake, either in a regular pattern or at random as the maker's whim dictates. One distinctive form of this type of trailing has become known as 'wishbone' or 'merrythought' trailing from its resemblance to the wishbone of a chicken (see Plates 11 and 16). The completely random trail which Thorpe has called 'snake-thread' appears to wind up and down round the body of the glass with the naturalistic effect which is itself a feature of Seine-Rhine glass.

In more extravagant vein, we occasionally find examples of 'flying' trailing that stands proud of the body (as in Plate 9) to create a rough effect of *diatreta*. However, such specimens are more often of eastern provenance.

'Snake-thread' probably originated as a result of the Syrian preoccupation with resemblance to birds, animals, and fruit, which is manifest both in shapes and decoration. Pieces with this form of decoration are seldom of a practical nature and represent the luxury ornamental glass of the period. Handles of trailing, often double threads nipped together at intervals or intertwined like snakes, are a popular form of this naturalistic style; and bird-shape jugs or bottles are relatively common, if one can apply the adjective 'common' at all to this particular form of glass.

The metal employed in the Seine-Rhine glass area was predominantly *Waldglas*, a metal in which the alkali content was provided by unrefined vegetable ash. As a result of failure (intentional or otherwise) to refine the component materials, the glass is generally green, yellow, or brown and gives a distinctive character to the objects made, creating a shadowy effect which has a beauty of its own and also provided inspiration for the modern glassmakers, particularly in France.

It should not be accepted, as has sometimes been suggested, that *Waldglas* is the creation of inferior workmen. As in every form of glass, inferior examples do exist, but much of the *Waldglas* we have is metal of a very high standard. What the critics generally overlook is that the makers have moved from an area of sunshine and impetuosity to a country of sombre nature and have adapted themselves accordingly.

That they knew how to create clear glass is proved by the window-glass, which was made in considerable quantities throughout the five centuries of Seine-Rhine superiority. Coloured glass is, after all, a fashion which comes and goes throughout history – in Britain it became fashionable under Victoria and has only now begun to lose its popularity.

The use of colour in the Seine-Rhine glass field was extensive. Coloured blobs of glass, either marvered into the body or standing proud, are an early form of ornamentation, the direct forerunners of the trail. Contrasting trails and coloured representations of birds and animals are almost as frequent as examples in self-colour.

Thus far we have considered only the development in the Seine-Rhine area, but other centres almost certainly existed in the west; Altare, near Genoa, and Normandy are both thought to have had some glasshouses even at this date. Certain minor differences in style are visible, but cannot definitely be set down as regional characteristics, and the style of the Seine-Rhine area may safely be considered to be representative of western European glass of this era.

In the east, meanwhile, the fortunes of the Roman Empire

were in a state of flux. The move from Rome to Constantinople (or Byzantium) was a logical one at the moment of history when it occurred, for Rome had by the fourth century become virtually indefensible and Constantinople was already a centre of culture and wealth, since it formed the commercial link between east and west. The impetus of the migration from Rome strengthened its position and introduced a greater degree of western influence than had hitherto been present. With the confluence of Roman, Greek, Syrian, and Alexandrian tastes and styles one might expect great achievements; but these were not immediately forthcoming, for the wealth of the Byzantine Romans provided an attractive prize for any alien power in the east, and not until the ninth century was there any security in the Empire.

The adjacent empire of the Persians became very much stronger by dint of minor conquests of Roman territories, and Byzantium was lured in the sixth century into a war which drained her resources and gave her little in return. The war between the two rival powers dragged on for the best part of a century, inevitably causing disruption of trade and cultural development so that, whichever side triumphed, it could only be a Pyrrhic victory. When the power of Persia was finally dissolved there appeared to be every prospect that the Empire would recover quickly, but with the disappearance of Persian rivalry came a new and more serious threat.

The Moslem religion obtained a strong hold on the people of the east in a very short space of time. To the cultured who were unwilling to accept Christianity it presented a palatable alternative; to the materialistic or barbarian the fact that conversion could legitimately be achieved by force meant material benefits to the converter. Once again, therefore, Byzantium was plunged into a protracted state of war; when, in the eighth century, she was at last able to repel the Islamic forces, we begin to see the growth of what can for the first time truly be called the Byzantine Empire. The next two centuries were marked by territorial recoveries and considerable prosperity, which was, however, doomed by the growth of other powers in the west whose development had been less restricted. The fate of Byzantium in 1204 was an inevitable one and to some extent signals the division between glass of the east and glass of the west.

The history of eastern glassmaking is closely linked with the fluctuating fortunes of Byzantium, for in the fifth and sixth centuries we can observe deterioration in the art. The mainly Syrian lines, which had been well established, gave way to a coarser type of glass, which some authorities prefer to call 'Arabic' and consider to represent a retrogression. It is true that some fine glass was still made as late as the middle of the sixth century, but it does not represent any advance, either technically or artistically, on the earlier Syrian glass. Christian glass with gold leaf was still made, and trailing and prunts were used with some success. War eventually deprives us of examples and there is virtually a hiatus before Islamic glass of the ninth century shows that artistic skill is far from dead in the east. It is not certain that Byzantium itself was a glass centre, but inevitably Byzantine influences can be found in Islamic glass of the ninth and tenth centuries – the term Islamic being itself used to cover most of the glass of the east. The glass of the ninth and tenth centuries shows certain characteristics which are new or revived. The art of blending glass of two colours with no definable change-over is revived – a direct progression perhaps from murrine – and shapes suggest that the metal is used more as a medium for ornament than as a utility. Bottles of exquisite shape but little practical use are common, and handles (where they exist) are generally inadequate. The use of enamel is brought to a fine art in the east – the west appears to have forsaken enamel at this period – and we can see the beginning of a style which will eventually blossom into the richly enamelled vases and mosque lamps of the thirteenth and fourteenth centuries. At first enamelling is sparse; eventually, however, the glass becomes little more than a base for the enameller's art.

There is a tendency to ascribe heavily enamelled glass to Aleppo and lightly enamelled to Damascus, but it is preferable in this case to assign the styles by date rather than place, because provenance is always confused by export, copying, and the exchange of craftsmen. The three pieces shown in Plates 23, 24, and 25 may belong to either centre.

The heavily enamelled mosque lamps of the fourteenth century are pieces which are generally beyond the reach of a private collector, because, although quite a number exist in museums, few are in circulation and the prices are astronomical.

Those in the British Museum are fairly typical and the beauty of such lamps in their original mosque setting must have been unsurpassed.

In the west, Christianity was becoming fairly widespread and political stability was virtually unknown; the result, as with many arts in the centuries between 800 and 1200, is that the continuation of glassmaking is supported by remarkably little evidence. We know that glass was made, for there are documents showing that window-glass was much in demand for church windows. In 758 Cuthbert, the Abbot of Wearmouth, wrote to Lullus of Mainz to inquire whether he could put him in touch with a glassmaker, and there is evidence of similar requests made both in the preceding and following centuries; but the main demand appears to have been for utility glass and not for luxury goods. Church patronage was lacking at the vital moment, glass having been condemned as unsuitable for church vessels; and continuous warfare in Europe drove the glassmakers to the well-established centres where a market still existed for glass in any form, however humble. In the ninth century there was a migration to Altare, near Genoa, which appears to have included many of the makers from Normandy and Picardy, for whom the depredations of Rollo left little prospect of trade in the north-west.

For further reference:

CHARLESTON, R. J. 'Ancient Glass-Making Methods', *Transactions of the Circle of Glass Collectors*, No. 124.
CHARLESWORTH, D. 'Roman Glass in Britain', *Transactions of the Circle of Glass Collectors*, No. 105.
HARDEN, D. B. 'The Achievements of Ancient Glass', *Glass Notes*, 16.
— 'Glass Vessels in Britain and Ireland AD 400–1000', *Dark Age Britain*, ed. Harden.
ISLINGS, C. *Roman Glass from Dated Finds*.
KAHANE, P. P. 'Some Aspects of Ancient Glass from Israel', *Antiquity and Survival*, Vol. II, No. 2/3.
KISA, A., *Das Glas im Altertum*.
MORIN, JEAN. *La Verrerie en Gaule*.
NEUBERG, F. *Ancient Glass*.
THORPE, W. A. See Bibliography.
YOUNG, R. S. 'Gordion 1956', *American Journal of Archaeology*, Vol. 61, No. 4.
And see Bibliography.

CHAPTER THREE

The Supremacy of Venice

WHILE Aquileia flourished there was little prospect of Venice rivalling her achievements; but when the fall of Aquileia drove the refugee traders to seek an alternative base the natural advantages of Venice afforded them an easily protected haven from which to continue what had hitherto proved a lucrative occupation in Aquileia. Venice, although little exploited at this date, was ideally suited as the entrepôt of the north-south trade route, and the refugees brought with them the commercial ability which had made Aquileia so rich and attractive a prize to the invaders.

Over the four hundred years that followed, Venice established itself as a trading power of far greater importance than Aquileia had ever been; by the time of the Crusades the ports were thriving and able to meet every demand; the negotiations with the Crusaders could not fail to enrich the Venetians, who, as sellers in a seller's market, exploited the situation fully. Thus, although there could be no enforcement of rights if the occasion arose, for military strength was lacking, they obtained trading concessions and wealth. Dissatisfied with the rate of expansion, the Venetians then took a step which may be considered indicative of their greatest failing. Venice supplied both sides in the conflict, with the inevitable result that the international goodwill which had been achieved was all but lost. None the less, the wealth that had been accumulated provided foundations firm enough for Venetian trade to withstand the stresses of the moment, and Mediterranean commerce found no suitable alternative to the excellent facilities of the ports of Venice.

In the field of culture Venice had adopted the best of the Byzantine (while paying little more than lip-service to Byzantine overlordship) as early as the tenth century, but the great cultural period was yet to come. We must therefore follow the settlement's history a little further.

An astute Government ensured that the ports of Venice were maintained on a scale which secured nearly all the traffic of the north-south trade route, and the wars which might otherwise have involved the Venetians were fought for her chiefly by those for whom she provided facilities. The fall of Byzantium in 1204, which benefited Venetian trade, was achieved without any effort on the part of Venice save to supply and encourage. Territorial ambitions were totally alien to the Venetians, trade supremacy being always the ultimate goal. In one instance, however, Venice had to fight her own battles; Genoa, by the early fourteenth century, had become a port of considerable importance and was making an uncomfortable impression on Venetian trade, thus infringing what by now the Venetians considered their rightful monopoly of Mediterranean commerce. With some reluctance, therefore, the Venetians took the appropriate steps and stifled the competition by capturing the Genoese fleet at Chioggia in 1380. Soon afterwards they received an unexpected benefit when, in 1402, Tamerlaine sacked Damascus and interrupted the overland trade route.

The supremacy which the Venetians had now secured would undoubtedly have been of greater duration had it not been for their lamentable relations with the other powers in Europe. The virtual monopoly of the Mediterranean trade route and the consequent tariff on international trade led in 1508 to the formation of the League of Cambrai; Pope Julius II, the Emperor Maximilian, Louis XII of France, and Ferdinand of Spain all found Venice intolerable; had there not been a certain amount of internecine strife within the League, it is probable that the fate of Venice would have been sealed. When the alliance broke up before achieving its object, Venice enjoyed some relief; but even this was short-lived, for the discovery of the Cape route by Vasco da Gama was already emptying the ports of Venice far more effectively than any political manoeuvre. Whether or not we should regret that Venice suffered this blow to her trade is doubtful, for Venetian trade supremacy declined as her artistic achievements neared their zenith.

Probably as a consequence of her international trade, or possibly because of the influx of the refugees from Aquileia, Venice had early acquired some knowledge of glassmaking. The documentary evidence reveals a thriving industry in the late twelfth century, and archaeological surveys make it clear that glass was common in Venice long before that, although its

provenance is debatable. Her contacts with the eastern Mediterranean were of long standing, and Byzantine culture had already
percolated through to Venice in the ninth and tenth centuries.
The fall of Byzantium may well have led to the increase of a
small glassmaking fraternity; the documents relating to the
thirteenth century suggest that the industry had received considerable impetus from some source, the most probable being
an influx of skilled workmen. In 1224 the guild of glassmakers
was recognised, and by 1291 the number of glasshouses was
such that the risk of fire on the Rialto necessitated an edict
compelling all glasshouses to be moved to the near-by island of
Murano.

The character of the early Venetian glass is unknown, but
it is probable that it resembled the Byzantine and Syrian styles.
Certainly the first pieces which can be attributed to Venice give
the impression of a developed art; earlier pieces, if they exist,
must be in accordance with the international vogue. The problem of recognition is rendered even more difficult by the similarity between glass made in Venice or Murano and that of
Altare, which attracted workers while Genoa thrived not only
from Normandy but also from Venice. This migration of workmen from Venice may seem strange, since there was an un-
limited market there, but we have already mentioned that
Venice had sought a monopoly of trade and she also sought a
monopoly in glass. To this end she sought to preserve the secrets
of glassmaking by forbidding workmen, on pain of death, to
leave the islands or to reveal the techniques of their craft. Working conditions may have been excellent and the financial rewards satisfying, but no artist can work for ever in a gilded cage;
the restless independence which haunts the glass industry urged
the glassmakers to move and they were not deterred by the
rigorous enforcement of the restrictions. We therefore find
Venetian craftsmen in most of the European glassmaking centres
from a relatively early date. The Altare glassmakers, having
never been subject to such restrictions, had already made their
influence felt in Europe, but the styles of Venice and Altare are
essentially so similar that it is not always possible to say exactly
whence the influence came.

We known that Venice was exporting glass by 1300, but it is
unlikely that such pieces could be identified, for it was not until

the introduction of *cristallo* (attributed to the Berovieri family, who were making glass in the mid-fifteenth century) that the glass of Venice began to develop individual character.

Cristallo, which may be regarded as the first real step towards production of a clear metal, was not in fact a different metal to that formerly produced, but resulted from the removal or treatment of more impurities. It had a distinctly greyish tint, but this could be disguised by the blowing; the colour is dissipated as the glass is blown thinner, although it is clearly evident in thick glass. It is probably as a result of this defect that Venetian glass has that distinctive thinness and lightness which contribute so much to its appeal, an appeal increased by the fact that a large proportion of the glass being made in Europe at the time was the heavy, coloured *Waldglas*; the early Venetian *cristallo*, of which the attribution is fairly positive, appears to have had no comparable competitor.

The limitations of *cristallo* were principally in the field of decoration after manufacture. Although the technique of diamond-point engraving was known to the Venetians, the metal was essentially thin and brittle – a defect common to most soda-glass – which may account for the limited use of this form of decoration, and the Venetians concentrated on those embellishments which could be applied during manufacture. In this respect they adopted and perfected many of the techniques employed by the Alexandrians, but they brought to these techniques the imagination of Syrian influence. At last we find technical precision and imagination married, and can examine the results which gave Venice her lasting reputation.

The early Venetian glass is notable for its restrained use of enamel, which is left to enhance the metal rather than overwhelm it, as was so often the case in Islamic glass. Typical of the early period are those vessels on which, in addition to normal enamelling, little spots of coloured enamel are applied to create the effect of gems set in the glass, and luxury pieces bearing armorial designs, which were executed with consummate skill, as can be seen in Plates 26 and 28.

This style of glass persisted throughout the period of Venetian superiority, as did 'chalcedony' (a refined version of the Roman murrine) and *millefiori* which, although well known in the Roman period, only developed as a precise art under Venetian tutelage. Since the Venetians mastered *millefiori*, this is a fitting point at which to describe briefly the process of manufacture. In Chapter One we saw how opaque-twist stems are made, and the manufacture of *millefiori* is not dissimilar. Composite canes are first built up of various coloured-glass metals, and then, the canes having been drawn out to the requisite diameter, cross-sectional discs are cut off and laid flat in a mould. Of course, one can use an infinite variety of different composite canes and build up complex over-all patterns before filling the mould with clear glass which fuses to the *millefiori*. The whole paraison can then be removed from the mould, and when it has been re-heated at the furnace mouth and marvered it can be free-blown like any other paraison. Alternatively, it can be blown in the mould or moulded without any blowing.

Perhaps the greatest achievement of the Venetians in the field of glassmaking is the use of *lattimo*, a milk-white opaque glass, which gave them the opportunity to display not only a superb artistic sense but also their complete mastery in handling their material. The early use of *lattimo* was simplicity itself compared with the later adaptations. We find bands of *lattimo* and clear glass alternated and drawn into wave patterns – the technique generally being called *latticinio*, although we shall find that this term is loosely applied to all forms of this work. The next stage was to make the white threads run in different directions (*vitro di trina*), and ultimately to form a lace network (*vitro a reticelli*), which might be further decorated by pegging air bubbles in the clear glass. It is extraordinary that the Venetians did not indulge in coloured *latticinio* to a greater extent than they did; apart from a few examples embracing red or blue, there is nothing to suggest that any colour other than white ever became popular, although the use of colour was frequent in other types of glass. One can only surmise that some convention restricted this obvious development.

The manufacture of *latticinio* poses some interesting problems, for any shaping of the metal risked distortion of the pattern and the creation of a dish such as that shown in Plate 27 involves incredible accuracy. It is not certain how the early *latticinio* was made; although we know the present-day technique, it has been suggested that this is not the original method employed. If one sought to make such a dish today, one would blow a long balloon with the *lattimo* running lengthwise, then twist the balloon and bring the two ends together in what would be the centre of the dish and then flatten the whole. The other way suggested is that two dishes are made, with the *lattimo* threads running in different directions, which are then welded together. Either method involves very considerable skill, and the nonchalance and speed with which the former process is today carried out is extremely deceptive.

With characteristic ingenuity, the Venetians, having introduced plain white canes, soon began to introduce bands of metal which were already made in the form of *latticinio* and the variety became endless. The use of the mould in conjunction with blowing is probably shown at its finest in Venetian *vitro a reticelli* of the sixteenth century, and the skill exhibited by its makers is not surpassed today.

Another form of glass particularly associated with Venice is 'ice-glass' or 'crackle-glass', which was developed quite early in the Venetian era and adopted later in most parts of Europe (see Plate 41). This is really an extension of the technique used to produce a glass form known as *semé d'or*, but, instead of gold dust, splinters of ground glass were used. The paraison was marvered on a bed of splinters, a covering layer of glass applied, and the whole blown. Alternatively, a similar effect could be achieved by the rapid cooling of the blown vessel, resulting in millions of small cracks, and then reheating to ensure fusion. Not many of the early examples have survived, because, although glasses made in the style would be attractive when new, they soon lost their lustre and became irreparably encrusted with dust.

The Venetian styles mentioned above were all adopted later in other parts of Europe, but perhaps the greatest legacy of Venice was the wineglass of the shape we know today. Until the Venetians began to make a feature of the stem between foot and bowl, most drinking vessels were little more than bowls on a flat foot with at the most a rudimentary stem – with the occasional noteworthy exception – and we must look at the developments of shape which both created and ultimately destroyed Venetian supremacy in glassmaking.

We have already seen that *latticinio* did not lend itself to complex free-blowing, and the early bowl formations and stems did not offer great scope to the glass-blower; plain *cristallo*, however, with its outstanding ductility, afforded every opportunity for the most intricate blowing and manipulating. The early bulbous stem, sometimes decorated with *mascarons*, or lion-masks, gives way to the highly elaborate winged stem, which in its early stages is extremely beautiful, and in its later stages is so exaggerated as to be neither practical nor in many cases beautiful; the glasses shown in Plates 29 and 30 are representative of the style. Throughout the period under review, however, the winged glass is notable for its extreme lightness and perfect balance. The latter feature is important, for the only practical way of handling many such glasses is to hold them by the foot with the fingers beneath. Winged glasses later gained great popularity in the Netherlands, and the technique of holding them can be seen in many of the contemporary Dutch and Flemish paintings. Few modern glasses have achieved the delicate harmony of design and physical balance of the early winged Venetian glass.

What began as a stem with 'knops' (rings or bulges on the stem) soon became an intricate snake-like winding of glass in which no central stem existed, the bowl being balanced, occasionally incongruously, on top of this mass of craftsmanship. From this point of history onwards the stem becomes the important feature, but at the same time as the stem was developing both bowl and foot had undergone radical changes. The bowl, which had hitherto tended either to be a long beaker-shape set direct on the foot or a shallow *tazza* on top of the stem, developed into an elegant conical shape in proportion to the stem, before, in the late period, the stem became so complex that no bowl could be in proportion. The foot became flatter and wider to preserve the balance and eventually adopted the shape we know today.

The stem shapes, which made Venetian glass supreme, soon became over elaborate, and the festoons and strings of plain or coloured glass (mainly blue) in the stem became so fragile and emphatic that they may partly account for the decline of the Venetian glass industry. The home market, impoverished by diminishing trade, would not support the impractical, and other glass centres were beginning to produce similar glass of a less fantastic nature; exports fell, also partly owing to the increasing fragility of the product, and the makers had to concentrate on the mundane to gain any profit.

Thus we find that Venice by the eighteenth century had dropped into a less significant position as a glassmaking centre; and, although Briati brought some ray of hope when he introduced the Bohemian techniques to Venice, the revival was a ray that flickered and died long before the fall of the Republic in 1797.

Relatively few complete examples of Venetian winged glass of this period exist, for obvious reasons, and those that do can only be dated approximately to the sixteenth or seventeenth century; but there is no doubt that Venice, in creating what is universally known as *façon de Venise*, has earned a notable place in the history of glass. We have dealt only with a few of the more definite styles of Venice; the Venetians also excelled in other fields, such as mirror-making and the production of paste jewellery and artificial pearls, besides producing the universal, indistinguishable variety of utility glass.

The ingenuity and artistry of the Venetians in the field of glassmaking is so widely recognised that the influence can still be seen in the modern glass of almost every south European country.

For further reference:

GASPARETTO, A. *Muranese Glass.*
HETTES, K. *Old Venetian Glass.*
PERROT, P. *Three Great Centuries of Venetian Glass.*

CHAPTER FOUR

The International Development

THUS far we have followed the mainstream of development
and noted the contribution of Venice. It is essential that
Venice should be treated separately, for her achievements
had far-reaching effects on the style of almost every glassmaking
country. We may now turn to those other countries in which
glass became an accepted medium and follow them individually
in their progress from their earliest efforts to the eighteenth
century. In some countries maturity has been reached only
recently and accordingly they do not figure here; the emphasis
must be on those countries which made a valid contribution to
the art at an early date, and mention will be made of those from
which a contribution might have been expected, but was not
forthcoming. Development in general follows one of two courses;
either the industry becomes established and produces an original
and distinctive style, or it concentrates on copying and lapses
into obscurity after a period of technical success.

There is one warning that bears stressing again and again.
Very few countries immediately develop a style of their own
and the attribution of any piece dating prior to 1700 to one
particular country should be viewed with a degree of circumspection; almost every country has at one time or another
adopted the *façon de Venise* and the utility glassware has a
universal style. This does not mean that attributions are impractical; in many cases extraneous evidence, the composition
of the metal, or the decoration will prove a good guide. Luxury
glass is infinitely easier to identify and therefore, in the summary
that follows, the characteristics noted are essentially those of the
glass one might find in the houses of the wealthy. There is little
doubt that some characteristics gained favour in the country of
origin only; therefore, at the risk of oversimplification, the
summary has been maintained at the level of generalisation,
save where some dominant style feature commands attention.

The reader will find in the bibliography works to which he
may turn if he wishes to study the glass of a particular country

in detail. Ultimately, however, the provenance of a piece can only be determined by comparison with other pieces, and no written word can act as a substitute for handling and observing. Here it is intended merely to show where each country fits in the over-all pattern of development.

GERMANY

In the context of glass-collecting 'German' is used as a descriptive term to cover a wide range of northern and mid-European countries to the east of the Rhine.

Almost as soon as an industry became established in the Seine-Rhine area, we find glass in most Germanic countries imported through centres such as Cologne and Aix-la-Chapelle and in the south from the trading port of Aquileia, but there is little evidence to suggest that much glass was made locally. When the Roman capital was moved to Byzantium the style of imports changed as trade began to move up the Danube; but, except for small glasshouses of limited duration, no real attempt to make glass can be traced until the end of the Dark Ages, when we find trade with Venice stimulating the growth of local glasshouses. The development of an industry in Germany is particularly interesting, for the propagation of knowledge can be traced to two fairly well defined routes, both starting in Venice. Moving northwards, we find a glasshouse established at Trento in 1468, in Halle and Innsbruck (1534), Nuremberg (1542), Munich (1584), and thence to Lauscha and Cassel in the northwest. The other line moves east to Villach (1468), Vienna (where there had been a minor glasshouse as early as 1428, but no real success until about 1480), and then branches out to Prague and Silesia. Thereafter the spread of glassmaking is less well defined and slower. This theory as to how the industry grew was first expounded by Wilfred Buckley and, while it has certain superficial flaws, the basic theory is now generally accepted.

The influence of Venice and the Italian glassmakers is, as one might expect, very much stronger in the south, but as the art progressed northward so the German temperament outweighed the Italian, with the consequent growth of a more substantial and robust style of glass.

Before embarking upon an account of German glassmaking

Black Sea

Adriatic Sea

Mediterranean Sea

North Sea

DANUBE

NILE

Aleppo
Damascus
Constantinople
Venice
Alexandria
Thebes

Potsdam
Lauscha
Prague
Nuremberg
Vienna
Munich
Innsbruck
Villach
Aquileia
Rome
Altare

Amsterdam
Cologne
Antwerp
Brussels
Liège
Aix-la-Chapelle
Baccarat
Strasbourg
RHINE
DANUBE
SEINE
Lyons
Nevers
Paris

Edinburgh
Newcastle
Stourbridge
Bristol
London
Dublin
Waterford
Cork

Kungsholm
Stockholm

Barcelona
Toledo
Granada
Almeria

Miles
0 100 200 300

it must be made clear that German glass is to be respected for the decorative techniques employed, even if the reader finds a great deal that is lacking in beauty of shape or perfection of quality.

The earliest local development, which dates from about 1450, is the *Maigelein* (or sunflower bowl), which is not unlike the Syrian palm-cup, with the centre of the bowl drawn up in a cone or kick such as one sees in a modern wine bottle; such cups were made of *Waldglas* in green, yellow, or brown. The majority of *Maigelein* bowls are mould-blown with ribbing or little super-imposed knobs, which, as we shall see, soon developed into a dominant feature of German glass.

We have already followed the development of the beaker from the low bowls, but the fifteenth century sees the emergence of a related and rather dramatic style called the *Stangenglas*, a tall cylinder often decorated lavishly with knobs known as 'prunts'.

The *Stangenglas* is a simple, essentially practical shape, but it is almost always impressive. The base of the cylinder is mounted on a hollow foot, and most have a lid – or have had one, for few lids now remain. From the true *Stangenglas* the next develop-ment is that the foot loses its importance for a time, during which the predominant shapes are the *Igel*, a squat tumbler with prunts, the *Passglas*, a long cylinder ringed with trailing and supposedly used for communal drinking (the rings representing the per-mitted measure), and the *Humpen*, which is little more than a cylinder. The *Humpen* and *Passglas* are illustrated in Plates 33 and 35.

A particularly Germanic development is the *Krautstrunk*, which, as its name suggests, resembles a vegetable stalk. These peculiar glasses, again cylindrical, were covered entirely with prunts and were favoured by no other country.

A close relative of the *Krautstrunk* (or, as it is variously called, *Warzenbecher* or *Nuppenbecher*) was the *Römer*; the pedigree of this shape is a long one, for it can be traced back to the 'prunted' *Stangenglas*, with the *Berkemeier* as an intermediate step. The *Berkemeier* was made by opening out the top of the cylinder to form a trumpet and covering the remainder of the cylinder with prunts. The cylinder is itself mounted on a foot which may be created by winding a thread of glass round a conical mould, like the old core-wound vessels. When the mould is withdrawn a fair-sized hollow foot remains. The *Römer* takes the process one stage further and draws the opened-out trumpet together at the mouth to form a bowl, of which the lower half is a cylinder and the upper half globe-shaped. Both the *Berkemeier* and the *Römer* were adopted by other countries, reaching their definitive proportions in the Low Countries. In Plate 38 the classic shape of the *Berkemeier* is shown, while in Plates 39 and 40 the Dutch *Römers* exhibit the finest characteristics of this development.

So much for the principal shapes, but it would be a mistake not to mention the seventeenth-century *Guttrolf* (or *Angster*), which is like a small decanter with its neck divided into three tubes, causing it to pour with a gurgling sound, whence it attained its name. These are not unduly scarce and have a considerable fascination. The *Guttrolf* illustrated in Plate 34 is typical, but examples do occur without the wide opening at the top.

The development of these shapes took the best part of two hundred years, and the metal in which they were made altered considerably during the period. The early examples are almost invariably *Waldglas* in green, yellow, and brown, and even late examples are found in this metal, of which the peculiar appeal endured even when good clear glass was made; there was no need to remove contamination or seed—their detraction from the appearance was minimal. But *Waldglas* was not suitable for the cylinders without prunts, such as the *Humpen*, on which the decorative techniques of Germany were employed to the full, and we find these in a fairly clear soda-glass of passable quality. But the quality of early German 'crystal' glass was not a prime consideration, for it will be seen that such was the desire to decorate that any merit the metal may have had was lost beneath the work of the artist. Only when we come to study Bohemian progress in the seventeenth century shall we see any marked attempt to improve the metal.

The decoration of German glass was initially trailing and prunting, but by 1541 enamelling was already a well-known art. Our ability to set a definite date to enamelled glass is due to the commendable custom according to which almost all early German enamelled glass was dated by the enameller. Although the process was probably learnt from the Italian glassmakers, the

Germans used a very much thicker enamel, which left a rather rough surface, but enabled the enameller to create a very much more definite colour. The popularity of enamelled glass was evidently immense: enamelling required glass free from prunts and the *Humpen*, of which examples are numerous, undoubtedly developed to answer the need for a broad canvas. The enamellers were in no way restricted by convention, for subject-matter ranges from imperial coats of arms to the most detailed portrayals of everyday life. Particularly favoured were serial pictures of various crafts, but the suggestion that such glasses were commissioned by guilds is in many cases clearly an unwarranted speculation – the portrayal is often far from complimentary. What guild would appreciate the portrayal of the cooper in Plate 33? German enamelling is often criticised as being a manifestation of crude peasant art, but this ignores the character of German civilisation of the time, which lacked the finesse of the Italians; it was bold and vigorous and expressed itself accordingly. Just as the preference for *Waldglas* endured, so did the desire for bold colouring; in neither case should it be assumed that the craftsmen could do no better. Subsequent styles of decoration show that the Germans had the skill to perform fine work, but they were always dogged by their determination to impress immediately rather than subtly.

So far we have dealt only with the particularly local style of German glass and its development, but in Bohemia there was perhaps greater sensitivity to the advances made by glassmakers to the south. The sixteenth century is notable for the rapid growth of an industry making glass in the *façon de Venise*; this appropriation of Venetian styles was, of course, not limited to Bohemia – few countries in Europe have not passed through a phase in which Venetian influence was dominant.

Nuremberg, which had first come under the influence of *emigré* Venetians in the early sixteenth century, was soon producing clear glass of good quality and also of a fairly distinctive style. Typical of the Nuremberg products is the goblet with a heavy straight-sided bowl resting on a tall stem made up entirely of collars and knops of various types on a wide, rather flat foot; often the bowl and foot were coloured. The style, although initially of elegant proportions, soon fell prey to the decorators, who saw in the Bohemian and Nuremberg goblets

(see Plates 36 and 37) a superb vehicle for their art. The basic
flaw induced by this adoption is undoubtedly the size and shape
of the bowl, which can be grossly out of proportion to the rest
of the glass.

Now it was not enamelling which smothered the glass but
engraving, and this is no matter for regret. The metal of the
day was not a happy medium for diamond-point engraving,
and wheel-engraving requires a strong metal of reasonable thickness which will not chip. Accordingly, research began in order
to improve the standard of the metal, and it was discovered
fairly early in the seventeenth century that chalk made the
glass more amenable to the wheel. This discovery was followed
by the substitution of potash for lime – which incidentally raised
the cost of production – and, in the late seventeenth century, the
introduction of lead, consequent upon English research. The
Bohemians now had what seemed a perfect metal, but they soon
found that, like early English lead-glass, it was subject to
'crizzling'.

Crizzling is a natural process by which incorrectly constituted
glass loses the ingredients giving it stability. If the process
continues indefinitely, the metal can, in theory, revert to water-
glass and will eventually disintegrate. Because it is a slow process, sometimes taking years to manifest itself, a great deal of
Bohemian glass of the late seventeenth century had deteriorated
before the fault was recognised and the remedy found.

In 1714, however, the balance of the ingredients was perfected, and the makers of the subsequent period produced glass
of magnificent quality. Much of the credit for the improvement
of Bohemian metal belongs to Johann Kunckel (1630–1703),
who, although a notable manufacturer of glass, was primarily a
chemist. He is best known for his development of ruby glass
using copper as the colouring agent, although he himself did not
discover the process, having learnt it from a fellow chemist,
Andreas Cassius of Hamburg. Hitherto gold had been used,
and ruby glass – once it became an economical proposition –
rapidly increased in popularity.

Most of Kunckel's experimenting was carried out at Potsdam,
where, at the age of thirty-nine, he was appointed director of
the Elector of Brandenburg's glasshouses. In addition to ruby
glass he developed fine transparent greens and blues and an

opaque glass called 'opaline'. This term is now used predominantly for opaque-white glass (*Milchglas*), but it then included all opaque metals. The discovery that potash, used instead of ordinary soda, made a clearer, less brittle glass is probably also attributable to the Potsdam glasshouses, but all these experiments may, in their turn, have led to the serious crizzling of the period.

The development of potash glass encouraged craftsmen to standards seldom attained since; and as the styles of drinking glasses became more elegant in other western countries, so did those of Bohemia. One concession to the changing styles was not made: for years the engravers had been accustomed to large surfaces and the large bowl remains a distinctive feature of Bohemian glass until well into the nineteenth century.

The great strength of the German and Bohemian glassmakers was undoubtedly the revival of old and the discovery of new techniques of decoration, which they perfected to a greater extent than any other country except Venice after the Dark Ages. An account of the glass of this area is inevitably equivalent to an account of decoration.

We have already observed the enamelling on early glasses, but from 1650 onwards a rival form of decoration appears which lacks some of the harshness of the early enamel. This was the painting of glass with an enamel wash, normally in black, white, and sepia, a technique whose earliest known exponent is Johann Schaper of Nuremberg, who was working in about 1640–60. *Schwarzlot*, as this technique was later named, lasted right through the eighteenth century in various forms and was adopted, to a greater or lesser degree, in most European countries.

The eighteenth century saw the revival of an old Alexandrian technique, that of inserting gold or silver leaf between two layers of glass. The two forms, known as *Zwischengoldglas* and *Zwischensilberglas*, require immense skill when used – as they were by the German decorators – pictorially or on a ground inner layer. Whether the result justified the care and precision necessary or not is a matter of opinion.

It has already been noted that the German metal was not particularly suited to diamond-point engraving, but when a fine, clear and intrinsically soft glass was developed there was little demand for diamond-point work, while wheel-engraving became by far the most popular form of decoration; perhaps diamond-point was too delicate in appearance for German taste.

Wheel-engraving depends very much on the existence of a suitable metal which will be clear and visually hard but actually soft enough not to chip under the wheel. Caspar Lehmann is the earliest recorded artist in Germany or Bohemia, and one example of his work is a fine beaker made as early as 1605; but it is clear from the standard of his work that this was no new skill. Thenceforward we have fine work executed on the relatively thin metal of the Nuremberg-type goblets, notable among its executors being the Schwanhardt family, whose engraving was generally polished to highlight the effect. But no heavy engraving could be applied, until the metal could be made thicker, without tints being evident, and accordingly it was in the early eighteenth century that the masterpieces began to emerge. When they did the pictorial type of engraving gave way to patterns worked meticulously, if rather elaborately, round a central detail; technically the work is beyond reproach. Cameo-relief was occasionally employed with a glass overlay, but the eighteenth century is above all the era of surface engraving.

HOLLAND AND THE LOW COUNTRIES

The area now to be reviewed may be regarded as the European melting-pot of Venetian and Germanic styles. Rich in Merovingian glass, the area certainly had a number of well-established glass centres prior to the Dark Ages, even though there appears also to have been a considerable import trade. Despite the fact that civilisation and culture generally lagged behind in the northern countries in Europe, it is clear that the standards, both artistic and technical, were higher in the Netherlands than in other countries nearer the Mediterranean.

As in almost every European country, a complete hiatus occurred after A.D. 800, which lasted there until the fifteenth century, when the demand revived at first for purely utility glass and subsequently for the other forms. The stages of development at first followed those of the German states closely, with the same beaker origins. All the German forms are found subsequent to the *Stangenglas*, and from the early paintings and woodcuts it is clear that only minor modifications were carried out. It is worth pointing out here that the documentation of glass history in this area is, throughout the period under review, remarkably well augmented by the paintings of daily life; few countries have such excellent contemporary and extraneous evidence of the development of the art of glassmaking. Of the glassware prior to 1600 there are few examples; but this is a failing frequently encountered where an industry can reuse its materials, as the glassmakers can use cullet, and where the development of fresh styles is fairly rapid.

By the beginning of the sixteenth century a great deal of Venetian glass was being imported into the area, and in 1549 the town of Antwerp, yielding to Italian pressure, gave a licence to a citizen of Cremona named De Lami to produce Venetian-style glass. The glass which thenceforward issued from Antwerp was notably Italian, but certain characteristics emerge, such as the adoption of the lion-mask as a form of decoration and the revival of the custom of inserting coloured glass beads into the body of the vessel; the beads were even superimposed on the prunt. The true Murano style succumbed to European *façon de Venise*, and this in its turn to the style more commonly associated with Altare, that is to say gadrooning and the imposition of applied work and finials. This tendency is far more pronounced at Liège, where the Bonhomme family controlled the industry, than in the more conservative glasshouses of Antwerp, but both centres suffered when their technical progress ceased to match that of Bohemia and England. Crystal glass virtually annihilated their trade and their products lapsed into a style which was totally undistinguished as early as 1725. The subsequent achievements of the two centres are occasionally confused with Bristol glass and a survey of their eighteenth-century products reveals little of importance.

Simple stems, with a central, teared knop, and engraved bowls are probably the earliest form of drinking glass, followed by moulded bowls and feet; a sapphire-blue metal predominates. Simple drawn trumpet bowls with some fluting, or short wide bowls on a folded foot with a stem of serried bulb knops, seem to be the standard drinking vessels throughout the period.

Openwork baskets, made of trailing and elaborately tooled, are often wrongly attributed to Bristol, particularly as the edges were often treated with blue trailing; it also seems probable that a number of Boot (or Bute) glasses come from Liège and not from England. The mediocre eighteenth-century products are so numerous as to present little challenge to the collector.

The centres of Liège and Antwerp have gained a mystique over the years which leads them to a position of undue prominence in the history of glass: their contribution is in reality limited. They do, however, represent the first step in the development of an industry in the Low Countries of any importance, and the later achievements were to come from glasshouses stemming from this source. From Liège the influence of the Bonhomme family spread over the entire area, and from 1550 onwards we find furnaces set up to form a comprehensive network from the extreme north to the southern and western boundaries.

In 1581 the area became divided as a result of the breakaway of the seven Northern Provinces. This independence of the north was further accentuated by Parma's capture of Antwerp in 1585. The result of this separation and the weakening of the Southern Provinces was to give a tremendous boost to the centres of the northern Netherlands, which increased in size, and multiplied in number, under an indulgent Government and the patronage of the prospering Dutch traders. Eventually the influence of Venice gave way to that of England, largely as a result of Ravenscroft's researches, which led almost immediately to an improvement in the Dutch metal. The standard of metal in the seventeenth century, even before this improvement, was technically high in relation to other European countries; although the metal bears a resemblance to *Waldglas* in some respects, the colour appears to have been intentionally chosen, since it is regular and controlled, rather than a consequence of contamination – and seeding is minimal. Clear metal of good quality could be produced, although most of it has a slightly misted effect, which at the time was virtually inevitable. The shapes of the seventeenth century which merit most attention are the universal *façon de Venise* and the *Römer*, which not only appealed as a basic shape but became in the hands of the Dutch a thing of beauty. The Dutch *Römer* is far less cumbersome than its German counterpart and loses the impressiveness, gaining at the same time a certain dignity. The failure of the Dutch to achieve greatness in the art of making clear glass in the seventeenth century is probably attributable to the dearth of natural resources. In the latter part of the century the import of coal eased the problem, but by this time the Dutch had discovered a field in which they were to have no rivals (save perhaps Nuremberg and Bohemia) for the next hundred years, and their attention accordingly turned to decoration rather than to manufacture.

It is not known for certain when the Dutch started to engrave glass, but the art which started as diamond-point or steel-point engraving, and later turned to the use of the wheel, was certainly well known by the third quarter of the sixteenth century. By this time it was a respectable pastime for the family to paint and diamond-engrave glass, and among the best work of this period is that of two amateurs, Anna Roemers Visscher and Maria Tesselschade. From the collector's point of view this undertaking by amateurs is particularly valuable, for it became customary on an anniversary to give a glass engraved with suitable sentiments and, more often than not, a date and the engraver's name.

As an art diamond-engraving had its limitations. It did not lend itself to particularly accurate work, but was ideal for scrollwork, drawing, writing, and doodling. Among those who took to it professionally was Jacob van Heemskerk of Leiden (1613–92), whose work was seldom excelled either in quality of manipulation or design. Again we have a craftsman who – at any rate during the later part of his life – signed his work, and examples are still fairly numerous; a short search of museum catalogues in England and Holland has revealed over twenty signed pieces and there are probably many more.

Diamond-point engraving, using a scratching motion, endured as the major form of engraving in the Low Countries until the early eighteenth century, when the Dutch challenged the hitherto uncontested superiority of the German wheel engravers. This latter form of decoration enables the craftsman to achieve a far greater contrast between the engraved and unengraved surface and thus the engraving becomes a dominant feature. However, the wheel has the drawback that it is less easily controlled than the diamond and error is obvious. The astonishing control exercised by the better Dutch engravers enabled them to execute work which, in view of the invariably awkward shape of the working surface, seems almost impossible. Acute curves on a sloping surface and the art of writing with the wheel in script rather than in capitals were achieved by the Dutch where lesser engravers reverted to the diamond. To Wolff (d. 1808) and Sang (*fl. c.* 1750), the great Dutch exponents of the art, such achievements were second nature.

Wolff, however, is more noted for his ability in another field, that of diamond-stippling. The discovery of this method is generally attributed to Frans Greenwood (1680–1761) of Rotterdam. The principle is exactly that of a newspaper photograph, the dots made by the diamond or steel points being close together or far apart to create shades and highlights. The rate at which this can be done, only one dot at a time, is of course very slow. Few people are known to have excelled in this sphere except for Greenwood, Wolff, and in our own time Laurence Whistler. That others followed the style in the Low Countries is certain, and attributions to Wolff and Greenwood are perhaps made more freely than the standards of the attributed works justify. The signature is a far less reliable guide than the standard of workmanship, which can be seen in Plates 69 and 71.

Enamelling was practised in Holland, but the quality of the enamels is poor, although the standard of workmanship is normally high. Certain English glasses, with a white enamel like milk and water, rather than the dead white achieved in England, may have been enamelled in Holland. The colouring of the opaque-twist stems in Holland is also of a less determinate white, a fact consonant with the lack of distinction of the eighteenth-century glassmakers. It is through their superb engraving that the Dutch are established in the industry; and, until recently, a great many excellent eighteenth-century Newcastle glasses were thought to be Dutch on account of their engraving. Such glasses are a happy fusion of the best craftsmanship of two countries.

The styles of the Northern Provinces tend during the eighteenth century to follow the lines of English development – scarcely a surprising fact in view of the community of interest in glass – but the bell and the large round funnel-shaped bowls endure in Holland when they have ceased to conform to the English concept of proportion.

FRANCE

Although France has a fairly continuous history of glassmaking from Roman times onwards, it has been an art ignored by modern historians, and indeed French collectors, until comparatively recently. Until James Barrelet wrote *La Verrerie en France* in 1953 there had been singularly little research into tableglass made prior to the nineteenth century and, the few collections that exist are far from comprehensive. This would seem strange were it not for the fact that the glass of the nineteenth century was so brilliant in its styles that, to some extent, it blinded collectors to the glass of the previous three or four centuries, glass which, with the exception of stained glass, can scarcely be described as either original or outstanding. None the less the history of glass in France merits attention, for the glassmakers spread through the country, even if they did not regard France as their journey's end.

The glasshouses set up in the west by Romans, or their trainees, continued to produce glass in the Roman manner until the development of the Seine-Rhine and Frankish styles began to influence the country. Although much of the glass is *verre de fougère* (glass made with the ash of bracken), the styles are those common to most of the Empire and the term 'Gallic' is more correctly used to describe provenance than to suggest an independent style. The spread of glass seems to have been northward and then eastward, the early glasshouses being found at Lyons, Strasbourg, Amiens, Rheims, and later along the northern coast into Normandy, with a somewhat different type emerging much later in the south and west.

There is very little glass dating from prior to A.D. 1000 which can be attributed with any degree of confidence to western France rather than the Seine-Rhine area; almost certainly there would be some importing and copying of Seine-Rhine glass.

The earliest mention of glass to the west of the Seine is in a letter concerning window-glass from Fortunatus, Bishop of Poitiers, to Rhadegonde, wife of Clotaire I, in the sixth century. In the seventh and eighth centuries we have appeals from the abbey of Wearmouth in Northumbria for workmen from France, but from this time until the fourteenth century there is a hiatus both in examples and informative documentary evidence, save in the field of stained-glass windows, but even here the documentation is scanty.

There is, however, a tradition that the industry in Altare, which has been mentioned in a previous chapter, was set up partly by workmen from Normandy; also Laurence Vitrearius, one of the earliest-known glassmakers in England, is said to have come from Normandy in 1226, so there must have been continuity of the craft during this period.

In 1302 we know that window-glass was made at Bézu-la-Forêt in Normandy, and in 1338 a particularly valuable document was drawn up by the Dauphin Humbert in which he granted certain timber rights and land to a glassmaker named Guionet to set up a glasshouse. The terms of the grant were scarcely generous, for Guionet undertook to provide nearly 2,500 pieces of glass annually to the Dauphin, who set out – to the advantage of posterity – exactly what the pieces should be. They include almost every form of household glass and the list gives us some indication of the industry's competence.

Both Charles V (d. 1380) and Charles VI (d. 1422) attempted to foster the industry, the former by exempting glassmakers from taxes and the latter by raising them to the ranks of the nobility; but their efforts were frustrated by the imports from the Low Countries, Germany, and Venice, which began to gather momentum during the last decade of the fourteenth century.

The fifteenth and sixteenth centuries saw mass migration from Altare back to France, particularly to Lorraine and Normandy, so that one might expect a thriving industry. Yet it was not so for long, for we know from the writer Bernard Palissy (1510–89) that the market was rapidly flooded and the art fell into some disrepute, with a consequent loss of craftsmen. One must also bear in mind the political situation of France in these centuries: continuous foreign war, religious persecution, and internal strife combined to restrain any development of the art beyond the purely utility level.

The domestic glass made between A.D. 1000 and 1500 must remain to a very great extent a mystery, but we do know now quite a lot about that of the sixteenth century, although examples are sufficiently rare to evade the ordinary collector. Predominantly it is crystal glass of the Venetian and Altarist type, often gilded or diamond-engraved. Having regard to the influx from Venice and Altare in this century, it is scarcely surprising that this should be the case, but the surprise is that certain local characteristics should develop as quickly as they did. Some of the sixteenth-century French patterns for glass have survived, and from them it is clear that the French developed a style of foot which bears little relationship to those of Venice or Altare. This is an inverted trumpet foot with a folded edge (as unrelated to the flat Venetian foot as chalk to cheese), on which stands a bowl of equal or greater height. Such glasses were not the monopoly of the wealthy, but none the less have a certain dignity, which perhaps accounts for the style persisting into the nineteenth century; there were also, of course, the more extravagant glasses which both in style and quality are comparable to those of Verzelini in England.

From the beginning of the seventeenth century the styles and technical achievements of France may be said in many respects to lag some years behind those of Germany, the Low Countries, and England. However, just as Germany had Kunckel and England had Ravenscroft, so seventeenth-century France produced a technologist of no mean ability; this was Bernard Perrot, who worked in Orleans from the middle of the century onwards. A great deal of his work followed similar lines to that of Kunckel, in that he researched into coloured and opaque glass. His individual achievements were more in the field of casting and moulding, but not enough of his work survives for any attempt at serious analysis.

Towards the end of the fourteenth century the French styles appear to follow the English with no clear time-lag – the sequence may occasionally even be vice versa – but during the eighteenth century the gap again widens; in technology there is at least a ten-year difference. Soda-metal was used long after lead-glass had been perfected in England, and tends to a brownish tint. On crizzled glass a peculiar pink tinge is apparent, which is met in few instances from other sources on the Continent.

To some extent the pink tinge was exploited when the opaque-glass industry flourished, the period covering nearly two centuries, but the tendency to attribute such a tint to Nevers should be corrected – the feature is too widespread to belong only to one centre, being common to most of the country north of the Loire. Opaque glass was popular in France long before it became fashionable in England – a reversal of the general trend – and the first half of the eighteenth century is conspicuous for some charmingly enamelled opaline of a type far more refined, both in character and decoration, than that of Germany.

The wineglasses of the eighteenth century should not confuse the collector of English glass, for the early period is represented not by baluster stems but by glasses of light thin metal, generally on a hollow, rather delicate, swelling stem with bowls characterised by moulded dimpling and fluting. The 'Silesian' stem of England is almost always elongated by the French, and appears in less restricted forms than the English version from about 1730 to 1770, when spiral stems became popular. These spirals were seldom executed as well as the English or Dutch examples and often rise from right to left (an almost unknown phenomenon in English glass), the pontil mark on the foot being ground down and polished. In England the pontil mark remained unground until the period of faceted stems which followed the spirals. Glass-cutting, although popular, never reached particularly high standards, being restricted in most instances to faceting.

From glass so lacking in originality it is therefore surprising that the nineteenth century should bring forth the outstanding art for which France is justly famous, but the last quarter of the eighteenth century just shows the beginnings of the mushroom growth. The glassworks at Baccarat and St Louis, among other centres that sprung up, were immediately successful in their copying of foreign styles. Much of the so-called 'Irish' cut-glass on the market today is, in fact, French, for at least eight glass centres in France are known to have imitated the metal, style, and cutting of contemporary Irish products during the late eighteenth and nineteenth centuries.

SCANDINAVIA

Although today we may regard Scandinavia as a glass centre, there is little evidence to suggest that there was an industry worthy of the name in this part of the world prior to the sixteenth century. The growth of the Scandinavian industry has been relatively swift, being helped considerably in the early stages by the abundance of fuel and materials.

In Denmark, Norway, and Sweden there have been found glasses of the Roman era, not only of the Seine-Rhine variety but also from the southern and eastern glassmaking areas, but the route by which such pieces came to Scandinavia must remain a matter for speculation. When the Dark Ages had passed we find Denmark and Norway, then united, importing glass from Venice and Bohemia, an import trade that lasted until the early nineteenth century, with considerable competition from 1700 onwards from England.

The first successful glasshouse at Nostetangen was run by the Norwegian Company, which was formed to exploit the natural resources of the country and concentrated eventually on glass production. By the middle of the eighteenth century, when it had been in operation for about ten years, the factory was meeting with considerable success; and by introducing English styles and German craftsmen it ensured that the success would be lasting.

The English influence was attributable in part to James Keith, who worked at Nostetangen, or the company's other works at Hurdels Verk, for about twenty years; but the variations in style make the products distinguishable. Combinations of baluster and air-twist stems are typically Scandinavian – such a combination being generally limited to simple knopping in English glass – although the metal and general appearance can, on occasion, be confusing. Distinction between English and Scandinavian air-twist stems can prove difficult and one must normally rely on bowl or foot shapes as a guide: the foot is often an exaggerated dome, which could not possibly be mistaken for the English variety. Engraving was carried out to very high standards, but enamelling does not appear to have been popular, although some forms of surface painting were tried.

In Sweden the industry began somewhat earlier, two Venetians being known to have produced glass in Stockholm in the mid-sixteenth century; but, apart from imports and early finds similar to those of Denmark and Norway, the first pieces which can be attributed with accuracy to Sweden are those of the Kungsholm glasshouse, which was set up in 1676, and the Skanska glasshouse, first noted in 1691. Both glasshouses were dominated by Germanic influence and the products tend to be solid and squat, with some good examples of engraving.

SPAIN

The glass of Spain merits perhaps more attention than is often accorded to it, because although the glass seldom achieves particularly high artistic or technical standards it is notable for the wide variety of styles which were adopted from other countries. Thus a representative collection of Spanish glass will contain the local version of Syrian, Islamic, Seine-Rhine, Venetian, and Bohemian; a study of Spanish glass, of which there is an excellent collection at the Victoria and Albert Museum, is therefore particularly informative, even if one's interests lie in other fields of glass manufacture.

Spain, at one time part of the Roman Empire, fell to the northern tribes as soon as the administration moved to Constantinople and about A.D. 409 the Goths and Alani settled in Catalonia. They held most of the peninsula until the eighth century, when the Moorish invasions established a completely different culture, which was to endure long after the Moors were driven out.

We know that glass was imported into Spain, and made in the Ebro valley, as early as the second century, but the evidence is so restricted that it is impossible to say more. When we next find evidence of an industry eleven centuries have passed and Islamic glassworkers are installed in Almeria and Barcelona, producing a very westernised version of the Syrian style. Trails, trellis work, and multiple handles abound, so that one is hard put to it to decide whether the north or the east has had the greater influence. In the early period of development the metal is generally green.

The industry evidently thrived in Barcelona, for in 1324 we find that the same risk of fire which had threatened Venice now necessitated an edict prohibiting glasshouses within the city. Even this, however, could not kill the industry, and in 1455 the glassblowers of Barcelona were sufficiently prominent to warrant founding a guild, Saint Bernardino being adopted as their patron. The industry was evidently encouraged, for in 1475 Isabella of Castile, the far-sighted patroness of Christopher Columbus and a woman of considerable intellect, allowed a glass furnace to be erected by the monks of San Geronimo de Guisando, which was to be exempt from taxes; it is incidentally a reasonable indication of a thriving industry that it could attract the attention of the tax-gatherers. Jeronimo Paulo, writing in 1491, tells us of an extensive export trade, which is mentioned again by Marineus Siculus, writing a few years later. The patronage of Isabella undoubtedly played its part in stimulating glass production, but the extent of her influence has become overshadowed by her less attractive activities in the sphere of religion. Barcelona however was by no means alone in supplying an ever-increasing market. Cadalso, in the province of Toledo, was noted in the sixteenth and seventeenth centuries for glass made in the Venetian style, particularly a form of 'murrine', and by 1700 glasshouses were fairly numerous. In 1725 the royal glasshouse of La Granja de San Ildefonso was set up; its products included glass in the Bohemian style and a particularly attractive white glass, which was often treated with permanent heat-gilding, allegedly the discovery of Don Sigismundo Brun. As we have seen above, Spain was subject to many influences, the east dominating the styles of glasshouses in Almeria, Andalusia, and Granada, while various western influences, mainly Venetian and Italian, are evident in the products of the other glassmaking areas.

The metal of seventeenth- and eighteenth-century Spain has a strange fascination; although it is full of seed and seldom free from colour, the workmen managed to turn a far from perfect metal into objects of interest and even of strong attraction. Symmetry was a minor consideration if the maker wished to show off some particularly skilful handling, but the glass can be somewhat stolid and unimaginative, or else extravagantly overadorned. Although the Spaniards had the opportunities to develop the finest glass in Europe, having the materials, the wide variety of craftsmen, and a considerable market, they never succeeded in producing work that properly meets the international concept of beauty. The absence of original creative power may be attributable to foreign conquests and religious persecution, but, whatever the cause, Spain produced little glass superior to her imports, appearing always to be experimenting. There is a tendency to display the various technical skills of the maker with little regard for the total aesthetic effect of a piece. The point is illustrated in some measure by the workmanship in Plate 45: although of a high standard it lacks the essential element of co-ordination in the design which could so easily have been attained.

RUSSIA

The glass of Russia is something of an enigma, for until recently little research has been carried out by local historians and some extravagant claims as to the distant history of the art have not been substantiated. It is regrettable that this should be so, for the prospects of obtaining evidence of early manufacture diminish continually, and the proposition that enamelling was an early Russian development is one which, if true, would cause reconsideration of the whole subject. The unsubstantiated claims, which came soon after the Revolution, have delayed and confused subsequent research to such an extent that only new archaeological discoveries are likely to verify the existence of any early glass furnaces; documentary evidence is lacking. A further difficulty is that research has been somewhat haphazard, and archaeological finds have been recorded in a manner which leaves the important issues in doubt. However, in the last twenty years a more accurate picture of Russian glass has begun to emerge as the result of the activities of a few determined researchers.

Most Russian art forms can be traced back to Byzantine derivation in the tenth and eleventh centuries; the earlier 'Russian' specimens of glassmaking which have been seen have borne an extraordinary resemblance to the Syrian exported glass found elsewhere. It is perfectly possible that Syrians did penetrate into southern Russia, but there can have been little incentive for them to remain and set up a glasshouse. The tribes of southern Russia, where one might reasonably expect to find Syrian exports, were scarcely of that degree of civilisation which demands glass in any quantity. Let the reader consider the standard of living and the social instability and then determine whether there was any place for a fragile work of art; almost certainly he will conclude that the Syrian would find little to attract him to the north.

Therefore, without denying the existence of a glass industry prior to Byzantine times, we can say that it is unlikely and that there is insufficient evidence to support an earlier date. It is perhaps more reasonable to suggest that Russia developed in this field at much the same time as Scandinavia (i.e. the seventeenth century), and prior to that date relied on imports for the small amount needed.

The greatest hindrance to the establishment of the industry in Russia was always the social order of the country. In many countries the occupation of glassmaking was respectable, almost to the extent of being noble, and there can have been scant incentive to foreign glassmakers to practise or teach the art in Russia, where the gulf between nobility and commoner was such as to leave little promise of social preferment.

The earliest evidence we have of glass made in Russia is dated to the seventeenth century, by which time there was a certain amount of importing of Bohemian glass. The market appears to have been limited to the court, and when glasshouses were set up their survival was of short duration.

The Tsar Alexius Mikhailovich (1629–76) made the first real attempt to establish a Russian glasshouse, and an inventory of palace goods of 1687 includes over 2,000 pieces of glass attributed to one Manio. Nothing more is known of this maker and no permanent industry appears to have ensued, although the date of the inventory suggests the possibility of some short-lived success.

Peter the Great (1689–1725) also decided that he must have glass and succeeded in attracting workmen to a glasshouse near St Petersburg. The failure of this glasshouse lies in the fact that glassmaking required a great deal of timber fuel and yet Peter himself – among innumerable other restrictions – made it a capital offence to fell any tree which could possibly be used for shipbuilding. The Empress Anna (1730–40) employed an Englishman called Elmzel to run a glasshouse at Yabino, which failed on Elmzel's death in 1738, eight years after he had taken over. The following years reveal several attempts, which all broke down as a result of imperial edicts.

The Empress Elizabeth Petrovna (1741–62) created a state monopoly of glasshouses in St Petersburg, but she forbade them to make glass for anyone other than her own court, with the inevitable but by now familiar result.

Really fine glass in the Bohemian style was made in Russia under Catherine the Great (1762–96), but again this industry had a short-lived success. The Imperial Crystal Factory, founded in 1777, continued with varying fortunes to produce fine glass until about 1900, but once more it was made exclusively for the court.

The result of this chequered history is that we have singularly little Russian glass, but what we do have is of the highest standards, made without economic consideration. Most of the examples we have are enamelled, and many bear coats of arms or monograms. They are all Bohemian in conception and their provenance must be undecided; it is clear that the court imported at least as much as was made for it locally.

CHINA

Perhaps the most realistic way of looking at early Chinese glass is to regard it as a precious stone, because its treatment owes far more to the lapidary's art than to that of the glassblower.

The earliest evidence we have of Chinese glass dates to the second century B.C. in the reign of the Emperor U Thi, but the earliest discoveries of the metal may date to any period in the Han Dynasty, who ruled from about 200 B.C. to A.D. 200, most authorities preferring to place examples in the latter part of the period.

Contact between Rome and China first took place in the reign of Antoninus Pius, whose ambassador visited the court of Yea Shi about A.D. 150, and it is probable that the rise of a small Chinese industry dates from this period, during which there was also a fair amount of trade with Syria. By the twelfth century A.D. we have good documentary evidence of glassmaking in Tchou Kow, but little is known of the nature of the products until the early eighteenth century. The Victoria and Albert Museum possesses two dark-blue vases, engraved in relief in Arabic, which bear the seal of Yung Cheng (1723–35) and another sapphire-blue vase bearing the seal of Ch'ien Lung (1736–95). All three are bulbous vases with a cylindrical neck opening out to a funnel and are in much the same style as the ceramics of the period; a further example in the Corning Glass Museum is to be seen in Plate 46. Also dating from this century are a number of snuff-bottles in green, yellow, and blue, with a dark overlay, carved in a way similar to jade. The dominant feature of Chinese glass is the use of carving and translucence for effect, and until the end of the nineteenth century it never developed as an individual art form, being always related to precious stones or porcelain.

As a field for the collector Chinese glass is somewhat limited, and the reproductions made in Stourbridge are sufficiently similar to confuse even those to whom Chinese glass is familiar. Perhaps surprisingly, Chinese glass does not command unduly high prices but it is always pleasing to the eye and often exquisitely made; it remains, however, one of the less sought-after varieties of glass.

AMERICA

The glass of America prior to 1800 has for the collector an attribute both unique and satisfying. In America, and America only, the initial steps of the glass industry are reasonably well known and documented. The story can be followed in terms of manufacturers as well as styles, and although the truly great achievements of the industry are of the nineteenth century, we can at last record the birth of a country's glass history in fairly accurate terms.

The struggles of the industry make a particularly interesting study, for it is reasonable to suppose that they are similar to those of the northern European countries to which glassmaking, as an imported industry, came late.

Seneca, in the first century A.D., wrote: 'In later years there will come a time when Ocean shall relax his bars and a vast new territory shall appear'; but his admirable foresight did not include the problems which faced those to whom the territory appeared. As has been said earlier, glass is normally one of the later facets of culture to appear, and it is therefore remarkable that the industry should have commenced as early as it did in America. Life for the settler was essentially rugged, and the prospect of emigration was one which would have little appeal to an artist or craftsman secure in a European environment, where the demand for glass was rapidly growing. Yet there were those who were prepared to try their luck, and we shall see that the path they chose was not an easy one.

The earliest American drinking vessels would be those of the English farmer, made from pewter or leather and essentially practical. Only when an element of stability and prosperity enters the life of the settler can we expect to find any demand for luxury goods. The first recorded glasshouse of the New World was at Jamestown, Virginia, where in 1608 a furnace was erected to make bottle-glass. There can be little doubt that the products of this furnace were coloured and similar to *Waldglas*, for there is no example of a clear glass made in America until the eighteenth century – nor would one expect to find the finest standards of craftsmanship among the pioneers.

The early venture was bound to be restricted to the most practical forms of glassware, and of these glass beads for trading with the Indians were the most in demand. The manufacture of these beads was a skill particularly practised in Venice, and it was no doubt from this source that the Virginia company sent over workmen to reinforce the infant and ailing industry in 1621. That they sent bead-makers is clear from the company's records and it is unlikely that they would be English, as glass beads had not achieved very high favour among the manufacturers in England at that time, while in Venice they had become a major branch of the industry.

The ultimate fate of the Jamestown glasshouse is not known, but it is probable that a shortage of craftsmen prepared to work under the constant threat of Indian aggression arose; and who could blame the Italian bead-makers for deciding that their prospects in Europe were more secure? Certainly the references to the glasshouse are extremely limited after 1621, and the last is in 1625. Perhaps this initial failure of the industry further discouraged any attempt at glassmaking until the political climate was more favourable, but some efforts were made in the seventeenth century to establish an industry at Salem (Massachusetts), New Amsterdam, and in Pennsylvania. Of these, the furnaces at Salem were undoubtedly the most successful, for they worked for thirty years, although frequently subsidised, producing bottles and window-glass. Of the industry in Pennsylvania little is known, although there is some evidence to suggest that Manheim, which was later to become a notable centre, was the site of two or three abortive attempts to set up the industry in the latter part of the seventeenth century. The only evidence of any glass other than the essentially practical kind being produced in New Amsterdam is a letter of 1658 mention-

ing a 'green decorated bowl of Ducking' (probably the manufacturer Duyckingk). Little is known of the activities in New
Amsterdam, but from the little evidence we have there must
have been a number of glasshouses operating there.

It is clear, however, that the larger part of the glass used in
the seventeenth century – the total amount being minute – was
imported from Europe, a trade of which the hazards must have
been numerous and the cost exorbitant. A long period of in-
activity follows the failure of the pioneers and it is not until 1739
that we encounter a man with the capital, initiative, and commercial experience to set up a successful glasshouse.

Caspar Wistar (1696–1752) had emigrated from Holland in
1718 and had met with considerable success in various business
enterprises in Philadelphia. Soon after his arrival in America he
had married into a hard-headed family of merchants; but,
although wealthy in his own right and by virtue of his marriage,
his egotism appears to have created social barriers and to have
antagonised those with whom he did business. Accordingly
when, in 1739, he decided to turn his ability to the manufacture
of glass he did so in a way which he hoped would give him a
virtual monopoly, regardless of others. The glasshouse which he
set up in Salem (New Jersey) was manned exclusively by imported Dutch craftsmen, bound by their contracts to work only
for Wistar. With the natural inclination to their own national
and other European styles, and a knowledge far in advance of
previous American progress, they were able to corner the glass
market with a new and exciting product.

At last we find the luxury goods in plain flint-glass that had
been denied to America for so long and the manipulation of
coloured metal, which in its American form is exquisite (see
Plates 122 and 124).

Green was undoubtedly the most common colour, while brown
and an extraordinary terracotta colour are now sufficiently rare
to command prohibitive prices. The range of goods made at
Wistar's glasshouse was vast and includes a particularly American phenomenon, which is a complete sphere, designed to act
as a stopper for a jug; the shape is commonly confused with a
witch-ball. The colouring of these spheres is in many cases
included to heighten the impression of mystery, for the control
of the craftsmen was of an extremely high standard.

As is usual, the success of one glasshouse led to the creation of others in the locality, and the closely guarded secrets of Wistar and his son Richard began to spread. The Whitney glassworks at Glassboro were started in 1775 by craftsmen from Wistarberg, as the area was now called (or alternatively Allowaystown), who found the Wistars' management intolerable. Richard Wistar lost interest in the industry after his father's death and maintained only superficial control over it, with a consequent deterioration of standards.

Few early glasshouses were able to withstand the after-effects of the Declaration of Independence and the imposition of taxes, and the once thriving industry of Caspar Wistar had long since forfeited its position of strength. From the wide variety of Wistarberg glass it is fair to surmise that the craftsmen were left a considerable degree of latitude in the matter of design, and it may be that a lack of industrial organisation, and the absence of mass production, played a great part in the decline of the Wistarberg glasshouses. Competition also played its part, for the activities of William Henry Stiegel must have caused the younger Wistar considerable concern.

Stiegel (1739–85) was another immigrant, but a very different man from Caspar Wistar. Within two years of his arrival in the New World Stiegel had selected his wife, Elizabeth Huber, the daughter of a wealthy ironmaster, and being both extravagant and extrovert he proceeded to enjoy life on a financial scale that did not accord with his ability to earn. In 1756 his father-in-law put him in charge of the iron furnaces in the town of Elizabeth; and there young Stiegel became interested in glass, just as in England a glass industry grew adjacent to the iron industry. In 1765 he set up a glasshouse at Manheim, which began by making bottles, but subsequently turned to flint-glass. The furnaces of Elizabeth undoubtedly paid for the furnaces at Manheim, but for a ten-year period—which was not noted for commercial success in other fields following the Stamp Act and Townshend's Import Tax—Stiegel ran the glass furnaces at full capacity, spending money as fast as he earned it and faster. He had little business ability, but adored grandeur, calling himself Baron Stiegel, having his coach drawn by twelve horses, and arranging for gun salutes on his arrival at his various residences, in all of which he maintained vast staffs in livery. After futile attempts to raise money, he eventually bowed to the inevitable in 1774; his glasshouse was sold and he himself was declared bankrupt. The man who had lived and distributed largess like royalty ended his days in penury in 1785. His multitudinous eccentricities were as fascinating as his glass, but are beyond the scope of this book.

The period of nine or ten years during which Stiegel's glass-house was working has provided us with some of the finest early glass, and a great deal of good flint-glass survives. The total output we know to have been vast and continuous, regard-less of the commercial folly, so that we have much for which to thank Stiegel. The styles are not easy to classify, but represent English, Dutch, and Bohemian without any particularly Ameri-can characteristics except in regard to moulding. The diamond-daisy mould (see Plate 123) and a softened waffle effect are definitely not European. His wine glasses are distinguishable from their English counterparts only by the flatter foot and the anachronistic bell bowl which appears in many examples.

The clear metal of Stiegel's glasshouse is of a standard far above that of most of his American contemporaries. Perhaps economic considerations prevented others attaining his stan-dards – the lead content alone would upset the economic balance of production. His glass consequently lent itself splen-didly to engraving and some fine examples exist. Stiegel's coloured metal was equally good and very different from the South Jersey *Waldglas*-like product of Wistar; a particularly fine rich blue or amethyst metal was used to greatest effect in the mould-blown glass. It has been suggested that he imported workmen from Bristol to make this metal, but, while it is true that the affinity of some of his glass to that of Bristol is remark-able, there is insufficient evidence to be dogmatic, since the production of blue metal was by no means the prerogative of Bristol.

The siting of glasshouses is so often regulated by the presence of an area of suitable fuel and materials that it is scarcely sur-prising to find another attempt being made to set up the industry in Pennsylvania. Coal was abundant and the silica in the area was ideal for glassmaking, with the result that once an industry was established it had good prospects. On a principle which Stiegel would have done well to follow, the early Pennsylvania glasshouses concentrated on window-glass and bottles, only turning to luxury goods when conditions warranted it. The earliest glasshouse – if we discount the abortive efforts of the previous century – appears to have been that of Gallatin, set up not far from Pittsburgh in 1786. The initial success of this glasshouse led to another being built close by in 1797.

There is some dispute as to whether these houses used coal as fuel exclusively, but from the relative freedom from seed of the metal it is reasonable to deduce that the glasses made there are the products of a coal-fired furnace which could be maintained at a high temperature. Wood-firing provides a far less constant temperature, and this can also affect the annealing. All the known eighteenth-century products of the Pittsburgh area are coloured.

New York also made an attempt to re-enter the market in the 1750's, as evidence of which we have various newspaper advertisements for bottles and flasks, but we also have records of the failure of the major glasshouse in the 1760's, through the absconding of tied imported artisans. Lee in Massachussetts was another centre that tried and failed, while Manchester in Connecticut had a limited success under the Pitkin family from 1783 to 1831. The Pitkin glass was practical, but of poor quality, perhaps largely owing to the continued use of timber as fuel. Whether its inferiority or a shortage of fuel was responsible for failure of the centre is not known.

Finally one must mention the Maryland glasshouse set up at New Bremen by John Frederick Amelung, who came from Germany in 1784. Amelung was a man of drive and considerable business ability who realised that one of the failings of earlier glasshouses was bad management. For eleven years he continued on sound commercial lines, producing some fine glass and engraving it with consummate skill (see Plate 125), but the demand for his goods was negligible and the works closed in 1795. Amelung was not to blame, for in any other country the magnificence of his work would have been recognised; but the people of America had perhaps not yet acquired the taste for such glass as he made and, like his inferiors, he failed.

It is not for any consistent reason that the early glasshouses faded, but one is tempted to the view that too often management was bad; and even the practical goods produced were inferior.

Perhaps initially the demand was limited or undiscriminating; the picture is one which must have been repeated time and again in other countries. Within the ambit of this chapter, however, one major achievement appears: Stiegel, operating barely 150 years after the art was introduced to the country, showed that fine glass could be made. It is a sad reflection on contemporary taste that no one apart from Amelung maintained his standards.

For further reference:

BARRELET, J. *La Verrerie en France*.
BEZBORODOR, M. A. *Glassmaking in Russia*.
BUCKLEY, W. *European Glass*.
CHAMBON, R. *History of Belgian Glass from the Second Century to the Present*.
FROTHINGHAM, A. W. *Spanish Glass*.
MCKEARIN, H. and G. S. *American Glass*.
POLAK, A. B. *Gammelt Norsk Glass*.
SELIGMAN, C. G. 'Early Chinese Glass', *Transactions of the Oriental Ceramic Society*, No. 18, 1940/1.
UMEHARA, SVEJI. *Ancient Chinese Glass*.
VAVRA, J. *5000 years of Glassmaking*.
And see Bibliography.

CHAPTER FIVE

The Birth of the English Industry

As WITH so many of the countries of northern Europe, the glass industry became established in England only after the upheavals of the Dark Ages had subsided. This does not mean, however, that no glass was made here at an earlier date; the Romans had occupied the country long enough for their art forms to be adopted in some measure. It is with some hesitation that one regards the piece shown in Plate 22 as an import, bearing in mind that it was found in Scotland, and there are enough fragments to indicate that glass was certainly a well-known commodity in this country prior to the collapse of Roman domination. However, we know that glassmaking, whatever industry there was under the Romans, became a virtually forgotten art from the seventh to twelfth centuries, for it is in these centuries that we come across the pleas to the Continent for makers of window-glass. We may assume that the pleas were answered, but it is also fair to assume that most of the workmen who came in answer to them returned to the Continent. Those that remained have left no evidence of their craft, unless it is the dateless and undatable glass in early church windows. Glass was not, however, the normal medium for windows at the time, and it is possible that when they were broken the panes were not replaced. No glass vessels are known prior to the thirteenth century, except for pieces that are quite clearly imports.

There is little reason to be surprised at this state of affairs, if one considers the foreign influences in Britain during the period between the departure of the Romans and the advent of the Normans: they were almost entirely northern European, coming from countries where glass was almost entirely unknown. What is surprising is that the Normans should have been here for 150 years before any glassmaking is noted.

The reintroduction of the industry, despite an earlier isolated reference to a glassmaker, is customarily attributed to Laurence Vitrearius, who settled about 1226 at an otherwise undistinguished hamlet called Dyer's Cross, near Chiddingfold, in the Weald. We know that Laurence came from Normandy, and suspect that he may have had connections with the industry in Altare; but no one has yet explained why he should have chosen to set up a glasshouse at Dyer's Cross. The choice can scarcely have been dictated by demand or supply of materials; Dyer's Cross was by no means on the current trade routes, and economic considerations can have played little part in the selection of such a site. It is just possible that there was already some local glass industry, fostered as a sideline by the ironworks then existing in the area.

Despite its location, Laurence's furnace evidently attained some repute, for in about 1240 he was commissioned to make glass for the windows of Westminster Abbey. During the first century of the furnace's existence the emphasis was undoubtedly on the production of window-glass, but there is sufficient evidence to suggest that already the market was showing interest in glass vessels. Both Laurence and his son, William le Verrir, enjoyed royal custom in some small degree, Henry III and Edward I both having glass in their inventories. Our knowledge of its source is limited, but we do know, for example, that Edward bought some urinals – glass bottles used by the medical profession for the diagnosis of complaints by examination of the urine – and, in the absence of other evidence, it is probable that these came from the Wealden glasshouse and resembled those of which fragments have been found on the site. In 1300 Chiddingfold received the Royal Charter, an achievement which owed much to the infant glass industry.

In 1343 the supremacy of Laurence's family gave way to the Schurterres, whose provenance is variously described as Normandy and Lorraine. Their contribution to the industry appears to have been less technical than mercantile, for, under Schurterre domination, the production and marketing were treated as two different fields, and we have records telling us a little of the activities of the factors, of whom the best known is John le Alemayne; his name first appears in 1332, while Laurence's family were still in control of the industry, but the records of his activities are chiefly of a later period. He acquired orders for glass for St Stephen's Chapel, Westminster, and for St George's Chapel, Windsor, while other agents found markets among the Oxford colleges. The success of the Schurterres lasted until 1435, when the Peytowe family came to Chiddingfold, and for the next 110 years the industry continued, without any notable expansion, producing moulded and blown glass vessels, window-glass, and doubtless other forms which have not yet come to light.

Thus for over 300 years the industry was ruled by only three families, all of whom chose to remain in the vicinity of Chiddingfold. When the centre of the industry does move it is the beginning of another era.

At this point we can turn from the history to observe the products of the Wealden glasshouses. These have been admirably treated by the late S. E. Winbolt in his book *Wealden Glass*, to which any student of Wealden glass will inevitably refer. It will suffice here to describe generally some of the pieces and fragments which survive.

The metal of the period is rather similar to that of the later glass of the Roman era, but is blown thicker. The colour is predominantly pale green until about 1600, when the Wealden houses turned to the richer green tint so characteristic of *Waldglas*. The decorative techniques employed were those of the mould and trailing. In the former technique the art was fairly well advanced by the time of the Peytowe family, for they produced wrythen moulded glass – we know this from reference to the moulds in the will of one member of the family – which requires experienced craftsmanship and is not normally a form connected with a purely experimental period. Trailing followed the pattern of other countries, spiral trailing being the most commonly encountered. It is in the shapes, however, that the chief interest of the period lies. The earlier Roman styles are recalled by broad-based vessels with tapering sides, the effect occurring in English bottles as early as 1400. This style, from the fragments we have, appears to have been more popular in England than on the Continent. There are a few fragments which suggest that the unstable form common in Germany in the sixth and seventh centuries regained favour (or possibly, survived) in England. The fragments correspond to the rounded end of a cone beaker, but, since footed vessels were already being made in England, it is perhaps a more acceptable theory that the pieces belong to a lamp of the type common in France at the time. The shape of these lamps is a globe open at the top and mounted on a hollow tube, sealed and so rounded off at the base that it is totally unstable, but may be held in the hand, or alternatively mounted in a bracket. Certainly such lamps were made in England, and the historical link with France is less tenuous than that with seventh-century Germany.

Fragments of glass of this period are by no means unattainable to the collector prepared to dig for them at the site of the early glasshouses; at least as much has come to light by chance as by organised digs. This is, however, a field more attractive to the archaeologist than to the average collector.

It has already been stated that the industry was showing little expansion, and until the third quarter of the sixteenth century development was slow in every respect. About this time, however, the art of glassmaking suddenly received a terrific impetus owing to the advent of skilled workers from Venice and Lorraine, who saw in Protestant England a friendly and virtually untapped market. Of these immigrant glassmakers Jean Carré was the outstanding figure, for he came to England having already worked in successful glasshouses in Arras and Antwerp.

Initially he came to the Weald, but he soon realised that London was the logical place for his glass-furnace, and, with the determination that was a major factor of his success, he made the advance for which the industry had been waiting. He may to some extent have been fortified in his decision by the dissension which his intrusion into the Wealden scene evoked. During his lifetime Carré was able to suppress the opposition, but when he died the Lorraine glassmen whom he had introduced met a barrage of hostility and pent-up resentment in the Weald, which led them to look for other homes. The principal cause of resentment was the expanding use by the successful furnaces of timber, the supply of which was required not only by the other glassmakers but also by the local ironworkers, who willingly joined forces to be rid of the immigrants.

Perhaps one should not altogether regret the fact that Carré's success bred resentment, for it encouraged the Lorrainers to spread their knowledge to other parts of the country and thus secure the industry. Our debt to Carré lies, therefore, not only in his establishment of the industry on a sound commercial basis, but also in his introduction of foreign workmen, who were not attached irrevocably to one centre.

The workmen whom Carré gathered round him belonged in the main to four families of Lorraine glassmakers, whose names were sufficiently distinctive to be traced after the dispersal from the Weald. In France, as in Venice and other countries where the glass industry was encouraged, it was customary for glassmakers to rank either with or just below the nobility and the names of *les gentilshommes verriers* were proudly maintained. The four families, their anglicised names set in brackets, are Hennezel (Henzey, Hennesse, Henty, Ensell, and possibly Ansell), Thisac (Tisac, Tyzack, Tissack), Thietry (Tittery), and Houx (Hooe, Hoe); their influence can be traced to quite a number of sixteenth-century centres by reference to local registers.

Members of the Hennezel, Thisac, and Houx families appear in Hampshire in about 1575 at Buckholt, and from there it appears that a move was made to Blore Park (Blower Park), near Market Drayton. By the early seventeenth century distribution was fairly wide and the names are no longer necessarily indicative of a connection with the industry; it is none the less probable that the families were still at work at some of the centres where the square Lorraine type of furnace was used. By this time, however, the Lorrainers had been augmented by other foreigners, and since Carré had connections with Germany and the Low Countries it is no surprise to find the occasional round furnace favoured by the Venetians, which had been introduced into Germany and thence to this country.

The Venetians brought to England by Carré were intended to produce and improve Lorraine *cristallo*, which he had begun to make in London at Crutched Friars; but, in effect, their advent destroyed the Lorraine style and replaced it with the Venetian. What Carré had apparently not considered was that Venetian technical skill could not be discovered at will from Venetian artistry.

By 1625 glasshouses were fairly numerous and the centres of Bristol, Stourbridge, and Newcastle upon Tyne were already tentatively established, as well as many others whose success was briefer.

The glass vessels produced by Carré's glasshouses, and their contemporaries, up to about 1575 are not easily defined, for only approximate dates can be attached to pieces and it may well be that many of his products are at present attributed to slightly earlier or slightly later craftsmen. From the fragments which can be dated to this period with some accuracy it is possible to discover strong similarities to the products of Lorraine and the Netherlands, the former contributing a domed or arched foot with a high instep, and the latter the slender beaker shape which under Venetian influence eventually rose on to a stem. Attempts to reconstruct or reproduce pieces from the fragments – notably the efforts of the late H. J. Powell – have given us a fair idea of the influences at work, but do not, of course, provide us with the detailed characteristics. The metal, in varying tints of green and blue, but sometimes approaching colourlessness, is on the whole of a high technical standard – although often marred by seed, probably owing to furnace shortcomings rather than any fault of the workmen.

When Carré died in 1572 his place was taken by Giacomo Verzelini, a Venetian who is believed to have come to Crutched Friars in 1570, when Carré was seeking to raise the standard of *cristallo*.

Verzelini was approaching fifty years of age when he arrived in England and, having married well and built up a successful business in Antwerp, had the confidence, competence, and financial security required to deal with the many hazards which he faced on Carré's death. By reason of his foreign nationality he was unable to own property in this country, and when the glasshouse at Crutched Friars was burnt down in 1575 (by a mysterious fire while the furnaces were out) the glass-importers, who were seriously injured by his success and may well have been responsible for the fire, must have believed that they would be free of this foreigner.

Suspicion as to the cause of the fire, anger, and characteristic determination led Verzelini to act with remarkable alacrity. Within three months of the fire he had applied for a monopoly to make 'Venice glasses' and a prohibition on imports for twenty-one years and obtained both; within the year he had become an English national. The glasshouse then earned him a fortune which enabled him to retire in 1592, a rich man held in high regard throughout the industry. In one respect, however, Verzelini may have failed to keep up with current trends: it is

clear that some time before the act was passed in 1615, prohibiting the use of timber as furnace fuel, coal was in relatively
common use. William Slingsby had 'perfected' the coal-fired
furnace in 1611, and the advantages of coal-firing were such
that even before this date there is admittedly ambiguous evidence in transport and colliery records which leads one to
consider dates prior to 1600. The introduction of coal-firing in
the industry cannot yet be dated accurately, but the possibility
cannot be ruled out that coal was available to Verzelini as a
recognised fuel. We know, however, that he continued to use
timber until he retired. This failure, if indeed it was a failure,
is regrettable, because of the resultant 'seeding' caused by
inadequate heat, but can perhaps be understood if one considers
the fact that his monopoly was limited, conversion would involve
extensive capital outlay, and coal was both more expensive to
transport and less plentiful than timber. As long as his products
sold well one could not blame Verzelini for resisting the change,
since the period of his success was foreseeably limited to the
duration of his monopoly.

Glasses of the Verzelini period are the first English glasses
which can be dated to within a few years, and the period should
really be taken not up to his retirement but to his death in
1606, since it is clear that, even after he retired, his influence at
Crutched Friars was not inconsiderable. It is no small tribute
to the glasshouse that we still have about a dozen pieces – the
first to come from a glasshouse specialising in table-glass and
not relying on that mainstay of the industry, window-glass.
They embody the best of Venetian skill at a time when Venice
herself was producing her finest glass, and are modified to suit
the temperament of a market that was both wealthy and discriminating. There is no southern extravagance in the designs,
nor is there the stolidity of some northern styles. That their
fascination is enduring and that their style does not date is
perhaps proved by the fact that a few have survived in new
condition. The 'AT-RT' goblet shown in Plate 48 is a worthy
representative of Verzelini's products and is complete.

The metal is grey-black or grey-green; seed has not in all
cases been eliminated. The glasses are lighter in weight than
appearance suggests and engraving is customary. The style of
the engraving is that common throughout Europe at the time,

being executed with a diamond-point in a series of scratches; it is in most cases attributed to Anthony de Lysle (or Lysley), the only known glass-engraver of the period. De Lysle came from France to England in 1580 and was noted for his engraving on pewter as well as on glass. It is unlikely that he worked solely for Verzelini, or even for one particular glass-seller; if he was not freelance, it is probable that he was brought over by the Pewterers Company, although his connection with them is only tenuous, but at least six of the known Verzelini glasses are engraved by the same hand, which obligingly dated some of the pieces. De Lysle was also adept at gilding and was probably responsible for the surface gilding on the 'Wenyfrid Geare' glass, which dates from about 1590; unfortunately the gilding is no longer clear, so that we have little knowledge of his degree of skill in this field.

Most of the Verzelini glass has found its way into museums, but a few pieces remain in private hands; on the rare occasions when they appear on the market they achieve prices commensurate with their rarity and beauty. A limited number of reproductions, obviously made with intent to deceive by Victorian craftsmen, are of interest mainly for their complete failure to match the metal or the artistic restraint of the original.

Our greatest debt to Verzelini lies in the fact that he gained his monopoly at a time when the infant industry faced severe foreign competition and was in danger of succumbing to the cheap imported glass. The standards set by Verzelini will be seen to have had the most profound effect on glass in England during the next two centuries, and his influence to have diminished the pitfalls of style which retarded the industry in other northern countries.

For further reference:

SALZMAN, L. F. *English Industries in the Middle Ages*.
And see Bibliography.

CHAPTER SIX

The Monopolists

THE period which follows the retirement of Verzelini is one of commercial and political chicanery. The business so firmly founded by Verzelini passed into the hands of Sir Jerome Bowes, a soldier of no particular distinction, who saw the prospect of making a fortune out of glass. He entered the business with no knowledge of glassmaking, but with an ability, perhaps born of his experience as Ambassador in Russia, to secure what he wanted – in this case licences and monopolies – by influence and intrigue, which must have been the despair of his rivals. His ignorance of the industry and the temperament of his workmen led to friction, for artists who know their work respond poorly to the military orders of a man totally out of his depth. In spite of the poor relations between management and the perpetually changing labour force, the influence of Verzelini endured for some while.

However, Bowes had paid dearly for his monopoly, which gave him the sole right to make and import all glass vessels. Although the monopoly was wider than that of Verzelini, he paid the Queen 2,400 marks for a twelve-year period, whereas Verzelini had paid nothing. In addition one suspects that he may have paid considerable sums in the course of acquiring the monopoly, for Bowes preferred to ensure a favourable ear to his requests at every level.

We have seen earlier that Verzelini's one serious error commercially may have been his failure to change over to coal-burning furnaces; Bowes had not the knowledge or foresight to correct this, with the result that although he renewed his licence in 1604, on less favourable terms, he found himself being squeezed out of business by those glasshouses which had converted to coal. Bowes died in 1616, having made no fortune out of glass and having brought to an end the influence of Verzelini by his contempt for and ill-treatment of those who had been happy to work under his more humane predecessor. It seems strange that one who had so little success as an employer should nonetheless be popular in the district round his glasshouses, but Bowes must have been held in considerable respect and even perhaps affection by the citizens of Blackfriars, who subscribed to buy him a warehouse in 1597 and, two years later, to rebuild part of his premises. Viewing the matter less charitably, one might consider whether self-interest induced the citizens to raise the capital.

The next milestone in the history of glass is undoubtedly the royal 'proclamation touching glasses' of 23 May 1615. We are told that like so many other countries England was finding the glassmakers' depredations in the forests a threat to the ship-building industry; since coal was available there was no reason why timber should be used any longer to heat the furnaces. Just how severe a threat this was to the shipbuilders is disputable; there were no power saws, there was a lot of timber, and no man cuts oak for firewood if there is anything else available, unless he wishes to expend a great deal of energy to obtain fuel. Another consideration, which perhaps carried more weight than is now customarily attached to it, is that a stockpile of timber stored close to a furnace, in the middle of a city built predominantly of wood, represents a far greater risk of fire than a stock of coal.

The industry had been hesitant to change over to coal earlier because of the difficulty in avoiding some degree of contamination of the metal by soot or fumes, but it is possible that Thomas Percival's discovery of a means of making the metal with minimal contamination (the crown covered pot) accelerated legislation; now there was little reason for failing to convert to coal, Sir William Slingsby having previously perfected a coal-furnace design suitable for glass.

After the expiry of Bowes's licence a patent was granted to Sir Edward Zouche which virtually restricted him to the use of coal, so he adopted Percival's technique without delay and by 1615 was already well established and prosperous. Although the proclamation would cause Zouche little concern, the year 1615 was for him the beginning of the end, for in that year Sir Robert Mansell joined the board. Mansell was then forty-two and already had a distinguished naval career behind him. At the age of twenty-three he was knighted for his service at the siege of Cadiz, where – possibly owing to parental influence – he had gone under Lord Howard of Effingham. It is difficult to assess what part Mansell's parents played in his early career – his father was a knight with considerable contacts at court and his maternal grandfather was the Earl of Worcester – and just how much he achieved on merit. By 1606 he was an admiral with command of the Fleet of the Narrow Seas and shortly afterwards he obtained the highly rewarding appointment of Treasurer of the Navy. It is likely that Mansell was a success as Treasurer, for his later business transactions are those of a born financier and not those of a sailor to whom finance was a necessary adjunct. When he joined the board of Zouche and Co. he found that finance and industry held far more attractions than the sea, and he arranged to be placed on the retired list. Like Bowes, Mansell knew little about glass, but Mansell had that hard streak and shrewd brain which marks the successful businessman. Furthermore he was blessed with an equally shrewd and competent wife, who ran the business for him with no small success when he was recalled to the Navy for a year to eliminate piracy on the North African coast.

Even before he was recalled to the Navy Mansell was quite clearly the power behind the throne at Zouche and Co., and on his return it was only a matter of time before he disposed of the rest of the board and assumed sole control. In 1623 the patent granted to Zouche and Co. was transferred to him by a new grant which gave him a reasonably effective monopoly in England and Wales. This was fortunate for the industry, because the 1615 proclamation had caused considerable upheavals among the minor glasshouses, and a strong hand, well protected, was necessary to consolidate the industry again; Mansell was just the man for the task.

The coal-mining industry in the Newcastle area was developed and coal-mining was started elsewhere to supply the local glasshouses; transport of coal to London by sea was organised; barilla – a vegetable soda at that time considered (incorrectly) to be essential for the manufacture of clear glass – was imported from the Mediterranean on a proper commercial basis rather than by haphazard shipments of small quantities, and the winning of clay for the pots was organised on a rational basis.

It will be seen from the above that Mansell was a man of wide vision and considerable drive who could and did put the industry on a proper financial and commercial footing; but, since he knew nothing of glass itself, the standards of the finished article were something of a mystery to him. There was not then, and there is not now, unanimity as to the quality of glass produced in his glasshouses. In 1620 Girolamo Lando, the Venetian Ambassador in England, wrote to the Doge and Senate praising the quality of the glass and saying that it was 'quite up to the standard of that of Murano' – high praise indeed from such a quarter. But in 1621 Inigo Jones was highly critical of the standard of plate-glass. This variation in opinion continues throughout Mansell's time and the truth is probably that standards varied very considerably from glasshouse to glasshouse and from year to year. Mansell was gifted with the ability to select able lieutenants and cursed with the inability to keep his men. In 1618 he secured the services of James Howell, who, though ignorant of the glass industry, proved to be an invaluable agent abroad and introduced Antonio Miotti, a Venetian then working in Middleburg, to Mansell. Miotti arrived in England with exactly the right qualifications, a thorough knowledge of glass, glassmaking practice, and the running of a glasshouse. But he was not qualified to deal with Mansell, who gave orders, like Bowes before him, in a manner more suited to the armed services than the somewhat electric atmosphere of a glasshouse, and treated his workmen with supreme contempt. Nor was the situation improved when Mansell went to sea again, because Lady Mansell proved, in this respect too, a worthy successor to her husband. In 1623 Miotti, like many another of his countrymen before him, left the Broad Street glasshouse and sought employment elsewhere. Eventually we hear of him again controlling glasshouses in Antwerp, Brussels, and Namur, exercising his talent with a freedom he had not known under Mansell. There he was able to keep his gaffers without a perpetual threat that they would be dismissed or leave.

Howell had left in response to parental pressure, and the constant flow of Venetian workmen which he had ensured was now arranged by one Mazzola, whom the Venetian Ambassador of the time describes as an 'irreligious and vicious rogue' – an opinion no doubt influenced by Mazzola's success in attracting glassmakers away from Venice. Attracting workmen, however, is not the same as keeping them and Mansell soon decided to obtain workmen from Mantua. These men he succeeded in keeping, which is not so much a reflection on the Venetians as suggestive that Mansell was beginning to learn something about artistic temperament. By 1635, however, Mansell had more or less killed the Venetian goose that laid the golden egg, and although the industry survived, largely due to the extraordinarily firm basis made by Mansell himself, no really notable progress was made in the period 1635–60, by which latter date Mansell had been dead for four years.

Before considering the type of glass produced in the first half of the seventeenth century, we must turn our attention momentarily to the industry in Scotland, which had really come into its own when coal-burning furnaces became accepted.

Here again we find the industry headed by a man of noble birth and considerable business expertise. George Hay (1572–1634) had been educated in France and had learned to suit his manners to his company to such good effect that he was able not only to keep his workmen but also to secure a monopoly in Scotland despite Mansell's formidable opposition. Both men were well versed in court intrigue, but no doubt the fact that Hay was a Gentleman of the Bedchamber gave him a suitable opportunity for requesting a monopoly; certainly he enjoyed royal favour consistently, for he was in his later years created Viscount Dupplin and Lord of Kinfauns.

Hay set up his glasshouse at Wemyss in Fifeshire, a well-chosen spot both for materials and fuel, and it was also sufficiently close to the sea to enable him to use sea-transport for the finished goods rather than entrust them to the appalling roads of the day.

Hay's glasshouse at Wemyss was a constant thorn in the side of Mansell, whose Venetians were only too anxious to leave; and Leonardo Michelli, Hay's London agent, was there to put them on the road to Scotland. Hay also obtained some measure of control in the coal industry in Scotland and proceeded to overcharge Mansell for his fuel supplies. Mansell's only way out was to negotiate a take-over, but Hay was not interested in selling to Mansell and when, in 1627, gout eventually prevented him from conducting his business he sold it to one Thomas Robinson, quite ignorant of the fact that Robinson was merely Mansell's nominee. It was, however, a hollow victory for Mansell, for the Scottish industry was still so much in its infancy

I Footing a wineglass. Note the overblow
between the bowl shape and blowing iron

2 The glassblowing process, showing the
chair and tools

3 Opening out the bowl after removal of the
overblow, using the spring pontil and pucellas

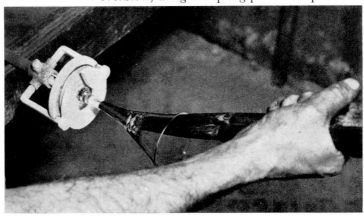

4 Model of a furnace described by Theophilus, the style belonging to the period 1000 to about 1400

5 Model of a furnace described by Agricola, in common use by the 15th century

6 Egyptian core-wound vessel.
About 1400 B.C.

7 Alexandrian pillar-moulded bowl.
1st century A.D.

8   The Portland or Barberini vase.
Alexandrian style. About A.D. 100

9   Green metal with flying trailing. 4th century A.D.

10 *Millefiori* type murrine. 1st century A.D.

11 Blue-green metal with merrythought trailing. 4th century A.D.

12 Honey metal with wrythen body. A phial of the 4th century A.D.

13 Amber metal with applied trail. A double phial. 4th century A.D.

14 Dark green metal with flying trail. 3rd or 4th century A.D.

15 Green metal with extruded trail. 3rd or 4th century A.D.

16 Almost clear metal. An amphora with merrythought trail in dark metal and dark handles. 3rd century A.D.

22 A clear green ewer with wrythen body. About A.D. 200. Found in Scotland

23   Syrian enamelled and gilded vase. Probably
Damascus or Aleppo. About 1325

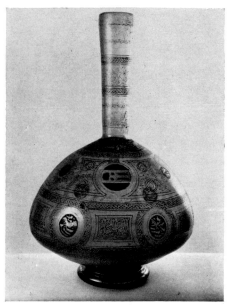

24 Syrian enamelled mosque lamp.
Damascus or Aleppo. About 1350

25 Syrian enamelled vase. Damascus or
Aleppo. About 1375

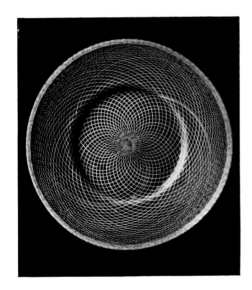

26 Enamelled armorial dish. Venice. Early
    16th century or possibly late 15th century

27 *Latticinio* (*Vitro di trina*) glass dish. Venice.
    Late 16th century

28   Enamelled goblet. Venice. About 1525

[*opposite*]

29   Winged drinking glass. Venice.
      Late 16th or early 17th century

30   A slightly later glass than 29, the central
      stem disappearing. 17th century

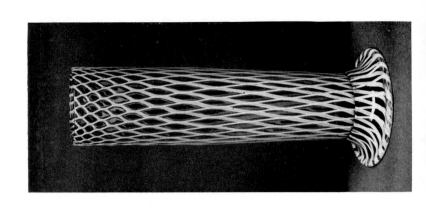

31 *Latticinio* vase or ewer with vermicular collar. Venice. 16th century

32 Vase or possibly *Humpen*. German *façon de Venise*, probably the work of an expatriate Italian. 16th century

[*opposite*]

33 *Humpen*, enamelled with serial pictures of the cooper's art. Note the activity in '10'. German. Dated 1616

34 *Guttrolf* or *Angster*. The rim contains a white enamel twist which is uncommon. German. Late 17th or early 18th century

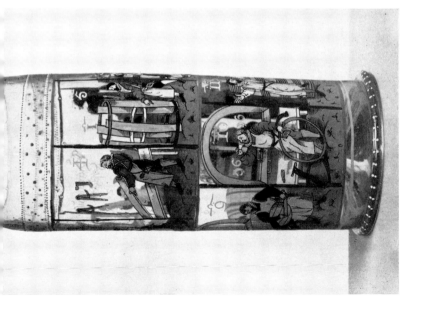

35   *Passglas*. German. 16th century

36 Covered enamelled and gilt goblet.
Bohemia or Silesia. 18th century

37　Engraved goblet with hunting scene.
Germany (Nuremberg). *c.* 1665

38 Diamond-engraved *Römer* of the
Berkemeier type. Netherlands. 1600–25

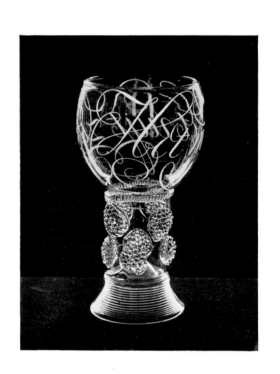

41   Ice or crackle glass with mascarons and a
bulbous mould-blown stem. 16th century

[*opposite*]

39 *and* 40   Two *Römers* of typical
    proportions. Both these glasses are
    diamond-engraved and represent the
    Dutch perfection of the German style.
    Late 17th or early 18th century

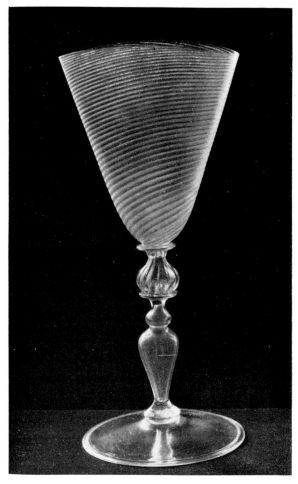

42   The adaptation of the Venetian style to the less flamboyant Northern taste. Late 16th century. Netherlands

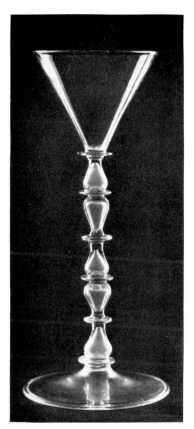

43 *and* 44   The typical Dutch development of
   Façon de Venise. Both mid-17th century

45   Cantir, from which the contents are
poured into the mouth without physical
contact. Spanish (Catalonia). 18th century

46 Giant Carved Bottle. Height 19¼ in. Red
overlay on white. China. Probably Ch'ien
Lung 1735–95

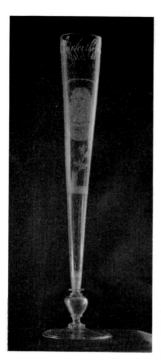

47 The Exeter flute, diamond engraved with a portrait of Charles II and the sprouting oak stump. The inscription reads 'God Bless King Charles The Second'. Height 17 in. About 1665

48 The Verzelini AT–RT goblet, probably made to commemorate a marriage. Diamond engraved and dated 1578. Only two other undamaged Verzelini pieces are known. English soda metal

49 Goblet engraved in diamond-point.
English, possibly Mansell glass. Soda metal.
Mid-17th century

50   An English glass Jug made by George
Ravenscroft. *c.* 1676–1678

51   The true baluster. Solid based bell bowl. Domed foot

52   The mushroom knop. Solid based thistle bowl. Folded foot

53   The true baluster over a crude annulated
knop. Bell bowl. Folded foot

54   A taperstick with honeycomb moulded domed
foot. Eight-sided stem and late in the period

55   Goblet with V bowl and eight-sided stem. Plain foot

56   Sweetmeat glass. Six-sided stem with
collaring at foot. Moulded and domed foot

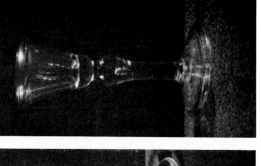

57   The angular knop. Solid based V bowl.
      Folded foot

58   The annulated knop in its later form.
      Solid based bell bowl. Folded foot

59   The simple knop. Solid based bell bowl.
      Domed foot

60   The inverted baluster. Solid based bell
      bowl. Folded foot

65 Wineglass with V bowl. Six-sided stem and folded foot. Early. Moulded pedestal group

63 Flattened knop over inverted baluster. Bell bowl. Folded foot. Note the decreased solidity of the bell

64 Simple shoulder knop. Round funnel bowl. Folded foot. A common form often attributed to the North

61 Simple knops. Trumpet bowl with solid base set on mereses. Folded fcot. The bowl shape is more common in the 19th century

62 Simple annular knops. Round funnel bowl. Folded foot

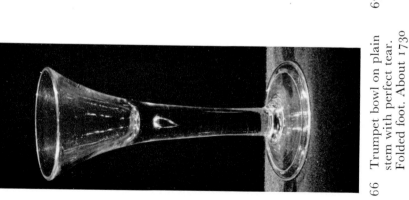

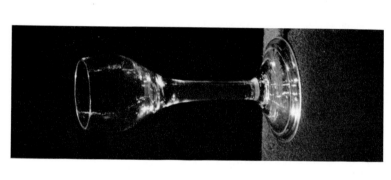

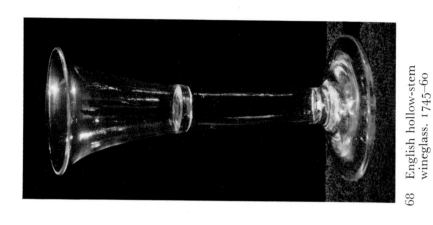

66 Trumpet bowl on plain stem with perfect tear. Folded foot. About 1730

67 Ovoid bowl on plain stem. Folded foot. About 1760–70

68 English hollow-stem wineglass. 1745–60

69 A typical multi-knopped glass with
domed and folded foot. Diamond stipple
engraved in Holland by Frans Greenwood.
Newcastle group

70 A goblet reminiscent of Dutch styles. Wheel engraved to commemorate a wedding in Holland and dated 1740. Newcastle group

71 A Newcastle light baluster wineglass of
about 1760–65, diamond stipple engraved.
The engraving is attributed to the
Dutchman David Wolff

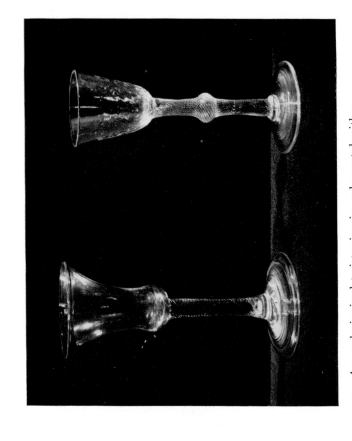

73   An early incised twist wine in soda-metal with a folded foot

74   A later and more refined version in lead-metal. The bowl is moulded and the foot plain

72   A magnificently made glass wheel-engraved to a very high standard. Here again the engraving may be Dutch. Newcastle group

75 Multiple spiral air-twist with Vermicular
collar at centre of stem. The twist
continues into the base of the bowl

76 M.S.A.T. with domed foot and engraved
bowl. The combination is unusual

77   An ale-glass engraved with hops and
barley. M.S.A.T. Folded foot

78   Corkscrew Mercury-twist. Mercury-twists
are generally restricted to glasses of this
or similar shape. 1760–70

79   M.S.A.T. bucket bowl wheel-engraved
     with vine motif. Domed foot

80   Corkscrew cable of spirals. Saucer-top,
     round funnel bowl. Plain foot

81   M.S.A.T. entering base of bowl. Swelling
     knop. Plain foot

82 M.S.A.T. Two swelling knops. Folded foot

83 M.S.A.T. Shoulder knop and more
angular central knop. Round funnel bowl
set on mereses. Plain foot

84 M.S.A.T. Four simple knops causing loss of
control of the twist. Waisted bucket bowl.
Domed foot

  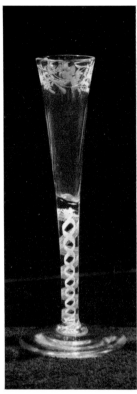

85 Multiple spiral opaque twist with saucer-top,
round funnel bowl and folded foot

86 Double series opaque twist with flute-moulded
ogee bowl and plain foot

87 Ratafia glass. Double series opaque twist.
Wheel-engraved bowl and plain foot

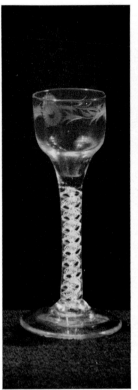

88 Double series opaque twist, the inner being a
    lace twist. Engraved ogee bowl. Plain foot

89 Waisted ogee bowl. Double series opaque
    twist. Plain foot

90 Pan-topped, round-funnel bowl, the lower
    part being slightly fluted and wrythen.
    Double series opaque twist. Plain foot

91   Norwich or Lynn bowl, here in conjunction
      with a folded foot

92   Waisted bucket bowl. The metal of this
      glass has a mauve tint—the result of excess
      manganese—causing the opaque twist to lose
      its brilliance

93   A Dram with ogee bowl and terraced foot

94 Ogee bowl and domed foot

95 Ogee bowl. Plain foot and knop at centre
    of stem enclosing Maundy coin of 1754.
    Wheel engraved with vine motif

96 Ogee bowl enamelled in white with vine
    motif. Attributed to the Beilby family

97   Colour enamelled armorial goblet, signed
     'Beilby invt. et pinxt.' The Arms are those
     of the Earls of Pembroke. Height about
     $8\frac{1}{2}$ in. 1760–70

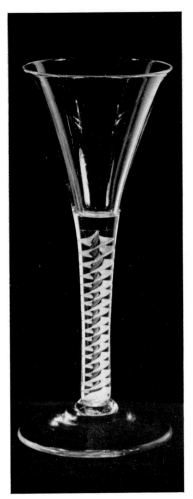

98 A white corkscrew twist with blue on the inner edge of the spiral

99 A central white corkscrew twist with an outer spiral of mixed white and chocolate brown threads

100   Firing glass with heavy flanged foot to withstand constant banging on the table

101   Toastmaster or Decorative glass with very thick walls and minimal capacity. Folded foot

102   Boot or Bute glass. Height 3 in. Small boots are not common

103   Dram with moulded bowl and oversewn
foot

104   An *avant-garde* style, popular in the 19th
century. This has a true firing foot and
the metal is certainly pre-1750

105   A toddy lifter of about 1780–90

106   English faceted-stem wineglass. About
      1780. The bowl cut and engraved. The
      foot out

107   The oak tree. The glass bears no other
      emblem and may not be Jacobite. Certainly
      not evidence of treason

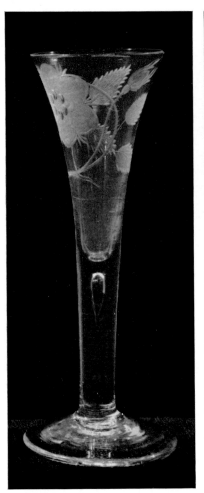

108 The Jacobite rose with one bud. Note the
unusual depth of the bowl. Plain foot

109 The Jacobite rose with two buds, the
oak-leaf, the star and the word 'Fiat'.
M.S.A.T. stem. Plain foot

110 A tumbler wheel-engraved with a
portrait of Charles, 'Everso Missus
Succurrere Seclo C.P.R.', 'Long Live P.C.'
and dated 1745

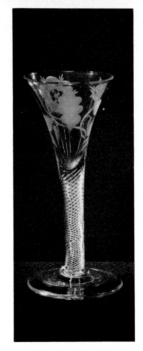

116 The Lochiell Amen glass. The bowl is
engraved with the cypher IR8 and two
verses of the Jacobite anthem. The foot is
engraved 'A Bumper' and 'To the
prosperity of the family of Lochiell'.

117 *Crystallo-ceramie* paperweight with blue
excised overlay

118   The Northwood vase reproducing a
frieze on the Parthenon in relief.
Typical of the reversion to the classical
styles

119   A jug typical of the Nailsea style. This is
probably true Nailsea

120   A Bohemian jug of the mid-nineteenth
century

121   A French vase made by Emile Gallé about
      1895

122 Pair of candlesticks. United States,
probably Wistarberg Glassworks. 1749–80

123 A deep amethyst flask. United States,
possibly from the Manheim works of
Stiegel. 1765–74. The diamond-daisy
mould is essentially an American feature

124   Covered sugar bowl. United States,
Wistarberg or Glassboro. Green metal.
About 1780

125   The Tobias and the Angel flip. United
States, New Bremen Glass Manufactory of
John Frederick Amelung. Dated 1788

that it required more nursing than Mansell had time to give it, and we know that he lost some thousands of pounds through his acquisition of the Wemyss glasshouse.

The glass of the Mansell period, for convenience generally regarded as 1615–60, is not as rare nor does it attract such high prices as one might anticipate. There are, of course, exceptions to this general statement and the finest pieces do fetch high sums, but two factors help to keep glass of this period fairly reasonable in price. First, much of it is practical glassware and coloured, and secondly, with the then current trend being to produce *façon de Venise*, it is often difficult to determine whether a particular piece is, in fact, English. The attraction of Mansell glass must depend on the criterion of the collector; while much is known of eighteenth-century glass, comparatively little is yet known about that of the early seventeenth century. Only the man who is prepared to make mistakes will add to our knowledge and this is a period in which scientific research is at least as vital as artistic appreciation.

What is known of the period enables us to divide the glass into fairly well-defined categories, which may be called green phials, bottles, green table-glass, and 'cristall' table-glass.

Phials, or as Mansell termed them 'violls', were functional containers for medicine or perfumes and the styles endured long after Mansell, just as in all probability they were established long before he came on the scene. Certainly they bear some affinity to the small Roman phials which were equally practical in shape. The height of the phials might be anything between 2 and 6 inches and the diameter from ¾ inch to as much as 2 inches. Their colouring is almost invariably green (iron contamination remaining), and ranges from quite a dark green early in the period to a fairly pale green by 1660. The degree of colouring cannot assist us in dating the glass within the period, for every glasshouse would produce a different colour depending on its materials and techniques; the general tendency seems to point to improvements in removing the contamination as a matter of course.

The shapes are fundamentally cylindrical with variations such as tapering or bulges, and decoration is limited to forms that can be applied by mould-blowing. The steeple-shaped phial, which has perhaps both the longest history and the greatest appeal, is decorated more often than any other – even so decoration is rare – and is almost certainly the most attractive shape for scent bottles. Chemical analysis of the interiors can be confusing, but at least one authority is prepared to say that the steeple phial is a scent container and not a medicine bottle. It is perhaps preferable not to rule out the possibility of the use of such phials for medicine – the style lasted in all approximately 350 years and must have become a rather monotonous cover for the exotic! Apart from minor variations in the cylindrical shape, a globe shape and a pear shape, the phial seems to have retained its essentially practical character.

The second class of glassware belonging to the Mansell period is 'bottles', a word which, in addition to its normal meaning, must here infer decanters. When Mansell first assumed the reins of the industry, wine bottle making was a comparatively unimportant part of the industry, for wine already had its recognised containers in wood, earthenware, and leather. The earliest bottles in glass of this period must have been decanters or serving bottles; all those which can be dated prior to 1640 are too light in weight and too thin to be intended for transport or as permanent containers.

In shape, the majority of the early bottles are either globular or domed with a neck of fair length – somewhat similar in proportion to a modern Chianti bottle. The metal varies from light green to virtually colourless (at least by the standards of the day), having developed from a fairly dark green over the course of some 100 years before Mansell.

The greatest achievement of the period in this line is undoubtedly the development of the practical bottle, which owes nothing in its shape to the styles developed for other materials. The shape is the simple globe with a long neck, which can be blown with ease by the least experienced blower, is thick and strong, and also pleasing to the eye. Whether the credit for popularising this container should be given to Mansell or the retailers is debatable; the latter were undoubtedly becoming capable of dictating taste, for in 1635 the Worshipful Company of Glass Sellers received a charter, which suggests that they were a reasonably well-organised national body, although the charter was not, in fact, ratified until 1664, owing to the intervention of the Civil War. The idea of a glass bottle for wine certainly had immediate attraction and what had hitherto been a mere sideline assumed a major importance to the industry. In the latter part of the century – after the Mansell period – the shape tended to be squat with a high kick in the base and a short neck, which would ease packing in bulk, but the result was much less attractive. Fortunately the latter part of the century also saw the birth of the lead-crystal decanter, which derived from earlier shapes and provided an alternative basis for future development.

In addition to crystal glasses at 10 shillings a dozen we find in Mansell's price list 'ordinary' beer-glasses at 4 shillings a dozen. These were quite clearly the products of the glasshouses that made the cruder bottle-glass, and although there is no complete example which can be attributed with any certainty to the Mansell period, there are some fragments which bear close affinity to the bottle-glass ware of the latter part of the seventeenth century. The shapes of the cheaper beer-glasses are not known, but there are strong grounds for suggesting that they were like the German *Römer*; the shape was certainly known in England. The form would be familiar to the imported workmen and innumerable fragments of seventeenth-century *Römers* exist in England – their origins being unknown – not only of the German type shown in Greene's patterns, but also of an anglicised form. Admittedly these date mainly to the period after 1675 in lead-crystal, but they are more likely to be the result of gradual evolution than a sudden change.

The 'crystal' glass between 1615 and 1660 is fairly well represented by fragments, but not by intact pieces. The blame for this must lie partly with collectors, for they have in the past sought pieces with an English character, whereas almost all the Mansell period 'crystal' is of foreign styles. This is not surprising, if one considers how reliant Mansell was on imported workmen, and one must look for *façon de Venise* glasses and characteristics normally attributable to Germany and the Netherlands. The earlier glasses of the Verzelini period have no definite English peculiarities and there is no reason to expect any radical change of style under Mansell.

From the numerous fragments excavated it is possible to state certain characteristics of the period which, it will be seen, are also current on the Continent. The *mascaron*, or lion-mask, stems so popular under Verzelini and minor variations in mould-blown stems survive for a considerable time. 'Mereses' (flat discs) and knopping appear, more commonly at the top and bottom of stems to disguise welding than as a decorative feature, and bulbous stems, occasionally wrythen or made in a series of bulbs, indicate perhaps the influence of the Netherlands mingling with that of Venice. Bowls of the half-globe shape endure and the bell-shaped bowl becomes more popular as time goes on. Occasional long flutes appear, the origin of which is almost certainly Flemish, and, of course, the beaker, now a great deal more elegant than its Germanic counterpart, is fairly common. Decoration is predominantly that of northern Europe rather than that of Venice, but occasionally a true *façon de Venise* winged stem is to be found. The metal is generally thicker than that of the Verzelini period and its quality less consistent.

By 1660 Mansell's organisation had disintegrated, the inevitable result of the Civil War and the Commonwealth period; Mansell's death was only the last step in the collapse, which had begun in about 1640. Although throughout the Civil War there was still the demand for glass, which the industry had sought to satisfy despite the inevitable difficulties, the period of the Commonwealth was disastrous. The industry responsible for the despicable extravagance of stained glass and the production of luxury goods to grace the imbibing of wine was unlikely to receive the blessing of the Puritans, and their iconoclasm may well be responsible for the dearth of earlier glass. When austerity excluded the production of fine glass, the great glasshouses were reduced to the low artistic standards of the bottle-glass houses, and no documentary evidence has come down to us of the existence of any successful glasshouse during the decade 1650–60.

The return of the monarchy in 1660 was the signal for art to advance once more, and within a very short period the glass industry came to life again. The Company of Glass Sellers, whose charter had never been ratified when it was drawn up in 1635 to protest against the deteriorating quality of glass made under Mansell's monopoly, received a valid charter in 1664 and thenceforward influenced both the artistic and technical quality of glass. Initially the Company imported Murano glass, but soon took to designing glasses for the English market and ordering them in Murano. Fortunately we know a good deal about this trade, for we still have the designs of John Greene, a prominent member but by no means the sole member of the Company to design glasses for the Muranese makers.

The importance of Greene is certainly exaggerated as a result of the absence of other designs, but both his designs and his correspondence may be considered representative of the trade of the day. About 400 of his designs are preserved in the Sloane manuscripts at the British Museum relating to the period 1667–80, a few of which are illustrated in Figs 2–7. Alessio Morelli, Greene's correspondent in Murano for part of the period, appears to have interpreted his instructions somewhat loosely and it could only be a matter of time before the glass-sellers realised that it would be more satisfactory and, in view of breakages in transit, more economical to make the glass at home.

By the time this was realised the industry was once again in a position to produce fine goods, largely owing to influential patronage and financial backing. The principal backer was George Villiers, the second Duke of Buckingham, who was persuaded by John de la Cam to invest £6,000 in the industry in 1660. Having invested such a sum the Duke swiftly obtained the patents needed by Cam and thereafter left the industry to its own devices.

There can be no suggestion that the industry did not owe a great deal to Buckingham, as much for his lack of interest in details as for his money, for Buckingham was entirely ignorant of the industry and never took an active part in its management, but he gave the industry the chance to regain its former strength in competent hands. Better-class workmen were attracted by higher wages and the period of 1660–74 during which the Duke backed the production of the so-called 'rock-crystal' is one of marked progress.

It was therefore to a thriving industry that the Company of Glass Sellers turned when they could no longer bear the vagaries of the Murano makers. The extensive imports had altered the style of glass considerably, for the long stems of Mansell's period, when made abroad, reached this country all too often prevalent in Greene's designs, but the stem had become a feature of quality glass and though sometimes only rudimentary was now de rigueur. This does not mean that every glass had a stem, for beakers, cups, and the Römer (still in its Germanic form) were made in considerable quantities. But the important

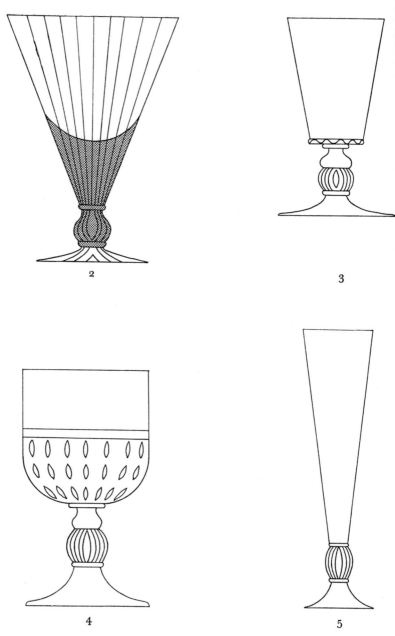

2

3

4

5

FIG. 2–7. Drinking glasses from Greene's drawing. *c.* 1670.

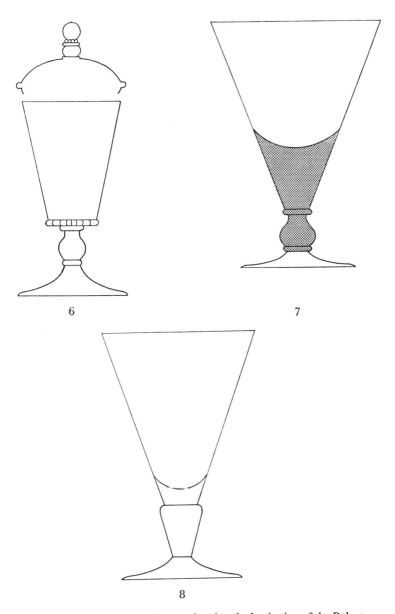

6   7

8

Fɪɢ. 8 Design, probably not by Greene, showing the beginning of the Baluster style. Contemporary with or slightly later than Figures 2–7 and attributable to the Glass Sellers' Company development is the simple stem in the form of a baluster, which might be either inverted or true. The bowl above is still a fairly simple shape; the V-shaped bowl, bucket (as in Plate 49), and round funnel bowls being the most frequent. The occasional long flute, essentially impractical but highly decorative, was set on a simple button stem, and the few examples of this basically Dutch design (see Plate 47) that we have are among the most attractive of the Restoration period.

Since the majority of these features also occur in the later lead-crystal, and in later soda-metal, the problem of dating glass to the Restoration period is tricky. Nor is it simplified by the fact that at least some glass-sellers, who were luckier with their opposite numbers in Venice and Murano than Greene, continued to import glass made to English designs. Whatever the provenance of glasses with features of Greene's designs, they are important, for they are all too few.

We now come to the discovery of lead-glass, if indeed it can rightly be called a discovery rather than a development of an existing principle. George Ravenscroft (1618–81) was a successful shipowner and international trader who had for many years been well known in Venice, where it is reasonable to guess that he first became interested in glass. His passionate interest in chemistry led him to experiment in glass and eventually his efforts attracted the attention of the Company of Glass Sellers. By this time Ravenscroft had set up an independent glasshouse in the Savoy, where he was making glass with a limited lead content; but lead was by no means regarded at this time as a principal component. Within a year of setting up the glasshouse Ravenscroft had found that he could produce a perfectly good clear metal which was unfortunately subject to severe crizzling.

At this point the Company of Glass Sellers realised that he was close to success and when he applied for a patent the Company found it politic to enter into an agreement under which Ravenscroft was to supply the Company with glass. It does not appear to have been final, in that Ravenscroft was still permitted to cater for others but, after a short period of satisfactory co-operation, a new agreement was drawn up in September 1674 committing him entirely to the Company. This was undoubtedly to Ravenscroft's advantage, for he was primarily a chemist and merchant and not an artist. The financial backing and provision of workmen and furnaces must have been wel-come. A new glasshouse was opened at Henley, where the research into metal continued, while the Company dictated the style of the finished products. One fly in the ointment remained: the glass was still crizzling badly.

In the summer of 1675 Ravenscroft must have discovered that the reduction in salts and increase in lead oxide solved this problem, for in September we find him authorised by the Company to dispose of anything made before August 'beyond the sea to Ireland or any other parts'. In other words, he was to dump the inferior goods! Crizzling was obviously recognised by the public as a defect of the Company's glass, for in 1676 we find a public assurance that things have been put right, and in the autumn of that year the Company found it necessary to identify Ravenscroft's superior glass with a seal. This does not appear to have been sufficiently distinctive at first, for in 1677 we first find the raven's head seal from Ravenscroft's own coat of arms on his glass; this seal was used until his death. The small jug in Plate 50 is quite clearly made after 1676, but before the raven's head seal became general.

It will be clear that Ravenscroft played a vital part in bring-ing England to the forefront of the industry and his achievements should not be minimised. It is true that lead was used in minimal quantities in soda-metal prior to 1675, but its significance as a principal ingredient was not appreciated, probably because a part substitution led to crizzling. The perseverance of Ravens-croft is therefore the all-important factor. It must not, however, be imagined that he achieved perfection, for the new 'flint' glasses had a considerably lower lead content than those of twenty-five years later. But his success led to a vast increase in the use of glass – not only the new 'flint' glass but also the old 'crystal' (i.e. non-lead glass) – with the happy result that although only a limited number of Ravenscroft's glasses exist there is quite a representative collection of glasses dating from 1680 to 1700. The styles associated with Greene and his fellow glass-sellers endured, but we can now see the development of a particularly English style, the baluster stem. Not only in drink-ing glasses but in other wares also we find this characteristic in both 'single flint' (thin) and 'double flint' (thick) glass.

'Double flint', a term which first appears in 1685 and is

synonymous with 'thick flint' of which we first hear in 1682, is normally accepted to mean that a double gathering was made before blowing. This is certainly suspect, for the new metal could be gathered just as easily as soda-metal and large amounts could be tooled before it lost its pliancy. It is preferable to regard it as a term to indicate thick metal rather than thin and not a reference to the handling technique. Alternatively, the names may be designed to maintain the trade secret and have no logical significance. The survival of single flint is due to the necessity of blowing soda-metal thinly and the conservatism of some of the industry after the introduction of 'flint' glass; it must not be forgotten that foreign workmen with memories of Venice, Altare, and the Netherlands were still a considerable force in the English glass industry. Both style and technique still lay to some extent in their hands.

On Ravenscroft's death in 1681 the Savoy glasshouse passed into the hands of Hawley Bishopp, who had previously been in partnership with Ravenscroft, and there is little doubt that some of the unsealed pieces attributed to Ravenscroft are products of the glasshouse under Bishopp. Ravenscroft's patent covered lead-glass for only a limited period, and so on its expiry every other glasshouse in London began to make lead-glass, with one notable exception. Henry Holden, whose glasshouse in the Savoy provided a great deal of glass for the royal table, refused to include lead in his metal – after all, it was poisonous – until financial considerations drove him to admit that people who used lead-glass did not appear to die any faster than his customers.

Where the Company were able to maintain control, the standard of the metal was high, but the provincial glasshouses produced a flood of poor glass which ultimately delayed their own progress, because whereas in the provinces the houses catered for the indiscriminate and their glasses crizzled, the London makers were improving the metal and rendering comparison invidious. The London glasshouses would not be over-willing to assist their provincial rivals and thus spoil the market, particularly in view of an early attempt to steal it from the London makers. It is notable, however, that Newcastle (1686) and Stourbridge (1696) almost immediately converted to lead-glass, and although their success was initially limited, both ultimately produced extremely fine metal.

It is a fair indication of the state of the industry that in 1695 the Exchequer saw fit to levy a 20 per cent tax on glass, to pay for the French Wars. No government would impose such a tax unless they thought the industry could survive it, and after four years the industry was still strong enough to win a long battle: the tax was removed. Had it not been removed, it is doubtful whether the industry could have fought on much longer and we might have seen the development of the English styles being virtually strangled in adolescence. They were now close to maturity and the approaching eighteenth century represents the golden era of English glass.

For further reference:

THORPE, W. A. *English Glass*.
And see Bibliography.

CHAPTER SEVEN

The Eighteenth Century: I

THE growth of the English industry in the last quarter of the seventeenth century coincided with the period of the Baroque style. By 1696 there were ninety glasshouses in production all over the country, of which, however, no more than twenty-seven were making lead-glass tableware. The demand for window-glass and bottle-glass was again on the increase, and some of the glasshouses primarily engaged in window and bottle manufacture produced crude tableware as a side line. It is probably from these houses that the English coloured glass originated. Throughout the eighteenth century, green glass tableware is known; blue is less frequently known and mainly in the latter part of the century, by which time coloured glass was becoming fashionable.

The Baroque style, in glass as in most other art forms, gave way to a classical elegance where proportion was the keystone, and extravagance gave way to substance. During the whole of the eighteenth century—which for convenience will here be extended from 1685 to 1810—the glass of England is free from superimposed glass decoration, relying on the metal and the tooled shape to create the effect. Gone are the wings of *façon de Venise* and the exaggeration of its devotees; gone are the insubstantial creations of the foreign craftsmen. In their place we have a distinctive national style emerging to suit the new metal.

The eighteenth century in England was a period notable not only for the development of styles, but also for advance in manufacturing techniques. This is all the more remarkable when one considers the tax levied on glass during the century and the expense of research and experiment in an industry where materials were becoming progressively more precious as tax increased.

The Glass Excise Act of 1745 taxed raw materials. Since 'cullet' was not included under the heading 'raw materials', it was not unusual for the glasshouses to enlarge the proportion of cullet so that it might amount to between a third and a half of the total batch. The result of the tax was therefore not as great as has been suggested by some authorities, and it is probably for this reason that the styles were not modified to any great extent, nor for any length of time. In 1777, however, the Government of the day, observing that the industry was effectively evading a proportion of the tax, altered the tax law to include 'materials or metal' and doubled the tax. Still the industry survived – inflation having made the act of doubling the tax less serious than it sounds – and increased, so that we find Acts of 1781 and 1787 again increasing the burden, in order to pay for the war effort. The final blow was the Act of 1825, by which the tax was related to the weight of the contents of the pot rather than the finished products. This was disastrous, for it meant that all waste material was subject to fresh tax and the entire batch had to be used to avoid production becoming totally uneconomical. The tax was eventually lifted entirely in 1845, with consequences we shall observe later.

Despite this severe handicap the industry made remarkable strides in the field of technology, of which perhaps the most important was the development of the 'lehr' or annealing oven. The principal figure in this field was George Ensell of Stourbridge, but he was not, as is often stated, the originator of the tunnel lehr. It will be recalled that, in the old furnaces, annealing was carried out in a chamber adjacent to or above the melting chamber, a technique which had two considerable disadvantages: the possibility of pollution and the difficulty of controlling the temperature so that the process was gradual. By about 1745 it was generally accepted that annealing could be carried out far more satisfactorily by passing the finished glass very slowly through a tunnel, one end of which was at working heat and the other at atmospheric temperature; the principle was noted as early as 1662, but does not appear to have found immediate favour. In this way even the thickest metal could cool at a rate which did not create stresses through uneven cooling of surface and interior; had the process been generally adopted earlier, the heavy baluster period might conceivably have been of longer duration.

By 1750 the tunnel lehr – the word 'lehr' being derived from the German 'lehr ofen' (an empty oven) – was common, although temperature control was a rather hit-or-miss matter.

The glass was drawn slowly through in a metal tray until it was withdrawn after several hours at the cool end, which would be about fourteen or fifteen feet from the hot end.

In 1778 Ensell designed a lehr in which heat control was vastly improved, and the introduction to England of the tunnel process is therefore frequently and incorrectly ascribed to him. The process is generally thought to have originated in Germany, but there is evidence that a not dissimilar technique was known in Venice at a considerably earlier date, and from one of these sources the process came to England.

It will be obvious from the decrease in seed found in eighteenth-century glass that the melting process also had been improved, a contribution made to the science by one Humphrey Perrott of Bristol, whose family appear to have been involved in the industry since 1696, not very long after it was introduced to Bristol. Perrott created a system of firing which is the basis of the modern blast-furnace, although it seems probable that he did not fully appreciate the extent to which his hypothesis could be developed. Increased heat meant larger pot chambers and better metal, but unfortunately development in the making of pots and materials for pots and furnaces did not advance at the same rate, with the result that breakdown was frequent until further research improved both pots and furnaces. Perrott received his patent in 1735, but his process was not generally adopted until much later. One of the snags which greater heat revealed was the production of lead oxide in such quantities that the pots suffered and corrosion led to impurities in the metal. Only towards the end of the century was this countered by altering the constitution of the pots.

Although as a result of technical advance the glass at the end of the eighteenth and beginning of the nineteenth centuries was heavy and of good quality, it belies the state of the industry, which was–in England at any rate–in a far from prosperous condition. The taxes had not applied, however, to Ireland and it is in this period that the Irish industry came to the fore.

It is wrong to consider Irish glass as a separate entity from that of England. Those who will dispute the statement are many, but there is no doubt that the craftsmen of England produced identical wares, although because of the taxes the heavier pieces are less frequent. The Irish industry was set up by Englishmen, manned by English craftsmen, and produced English styles. Confident attribution, save in a few instances where cutting embraces features popular in Ireland only, should be regarded with circumspection, and unless the piece is marked it is exceptionally unusual to be able to say from which glasshouse any given piece may have come. Hartshorne, who originated the myth of 'blue' Waterford, did a considerable disservice, since blue is one of the commoner tints, caused either by the lead content or by impurities such as copper or iron, and is particularly common in French glass of the late eighteenth and early nineteenth centuries. It is a myth perpetuated and exploited by the unscrupulous, although created in the utmost good faith, and one which cannot be justified in the light of current knowledge.

With this caveat firmly in mind let us consider the industry in Ireland and its achievements. There is a record of a grant of land in Dublin to a glassmaker in 1258, but no evidence of any glasshouse until 1585. Except that it existed, we know nothing of this glasshouse, and it is only in the late eighteenth century that the industry really made progress, after the imposition in England of the heavy duty and the grant of free trade to Ireland. In order to minimise false attributions the dates are given below at which some of the glasshouses were set up.

1691 Dublin: An established glasshouse taken over by Philip Roche. No marked pieces.

1729 Kilkenny: This enterprise failed in 1740. No marked pieces.

1761 Cork: Evidence of an infant industry. No marked pieces.

1771 Drunrea: Benjamin Edwards of Bristol. No marked pieces.

1776 Belfast: Benjamin Edwards moved. Pieces marked by moulded lettering on base 'B. Edwards Belfast'.

1783 Cork: Hayes Burnett and Rowe set up the Cork Glass Company. Pieces marked 'Cork Glass Company' or 'Cork Glass Co.'

1783 Waterford: The Penrose Brothers and John Hill of Stourbridge. Pieces marked 'Penrose Waterford'.

1785 Dublin: Charles Mulvaney. Pieces marked 'C. M. Co.'

1799 Dublin: J. D. Ayckbower. Pieces marked 'J. D. Ayckbower Dublin' or 'Ayckbower Dublin'.

1818 Cork: Waterloo Glass Company. Pieces marked 'Waterloo Company Cork' or 'Waterloo Co. Cork'.

This short catalogue is clearly far from complete. We know
that there was a glasshouse flourishing in Dungannon prior to
1783, but the facts available do not permit any certain date to
be given. In all cases marked pieces are the exception, and
naturally enough have attracted the forgers. Between 1836 when
the Waterloo Glass Company failed and 1845 when the excise
duty (imposed in 1825) was removed, there is an extraordinary
hiatus in production, although Cork achieved a reputation for
cutting glass made elsewhere.

It is dangerous to attempt to define characteristics of Irish
glass, but certain features were more popular with the Irish
glassmakers than with their English counterparts. Shapes favoured in Ireland were the oval and boat shape which found
their optimum expression in such pieces as fruit-bowls and salt-
cellars. The diamond-shaped foot was more common in Ireland,
being most suited in proportion to a bowl of either boat or oval
contour. Heavy pieces are more frequent, for it is in this respect
that the freedom from duty gave the greatest advantage. In
pieces of more usual shape the edge of a bowl may be turned
over to give a rounded top surface and the down-turned edge
left plain or cut.

Since the Irish industry only gathered momentum at a time
when cutting was becoming fashionable, and cutting requires
a good thickness of metal, it would be surprising if the Irish
makers had not developed the art of cutting to a high standard.
Apart from the standard forms of cutting employed in England,
some styles are almost certainly Irish in origin. The serrated
edge appears early in the period, closely followed by the Van
Dyck edge (shaped like the lace collars in Flemish portraits).
Lozenge-cutting appears by about 1790 and step-cutting within
the following ten or fifteen years. Notch-cutting, which was not
common in England at this period, was used in Ireland, but even
here it is less frequent than its ease of execution might lead one
to expect. Pillar flute cutting was adopted, so far as can be
ascertained, only by Waterford, and apart from markings this
is the sole indication of provenance.

The meteoric rise of the Irish industry and its almost equally rapid decline are attributable to the incidence of the excise duty. The products of the period ensured, however, that a re-birth of the industry would not be long in coming, for their quality both in metal and craftsmanship had created a reputation which Ireland has never lost. Although it is in the field of cutting that Irish glass first came to the fore, the other products of the Irish houses are not to be dismissed as insignificant; they are just not easily distinguished from their English contemporaries.

For the collector, the eighteenth century is the golden era of English glass, for the metal at last reaches a status level with silver and porcelain and becomes the accepted medium for drinking vessels. When one considers the number of drinking glasses extant, it is clear that there can have been no small demand for them in the period, and fortunately the drinking glasses reflect the changing fashions of the century so accurately that they tend to eclipse other glass forms.

The major difficulty facing early writers was the lack of unanimity in describing the various shapes, but this difficulty has been resolved to a very great extent by E. Barrington Haynes, who set out in *Glass through the Ages* to reach a definitive system, which is gradually becoming universal. The shapes described and illustrated here are in accordance with Haynes's definitions, and the reader is encouraged to adopt them and to require dealers' descriptions to accord with Haynes's system. In this way he will serve both himself and others. The shapes and classification will be recognised by reference to the Figures on pages 163–168 and the illustrations.

The only satisfactory classification of drinking glasses of the period is by reference to the stem formation, and again the analytical mind of Haynes evolved the most satisfactory method. He divided the glasses into thirteen groups.

Group   I Baluster Stems 1685–1725
           II Moulded Pedestal Stems 1715–65
     III Balustroid Stems 1725–60
     IV Light (Newcastle) Balusters 1735–65
      V Composite Stems 1745–75
     VI Plain Straight Stems 1740–75
    VII Air-Twist Stems 1745–70

VIII   Hollow Stems 1750–60
  IX   Incised Twist Stems 1750–65
   X   Opaque-White Twist Stems 1755–80
  XI   Mixed and Colour-Twist Stems 1755–75
 XII   Faceted Stems 1760–1810
XIII   Other glasses with rudimentary stems

Naturally there are limitations to any definitive grouping by date, in that it caters neither for the *avant-garde* nor the conservative extremes. The author is at variance with Haynes's dating, but this in no way derogates from the system of classification adopted by the latter.

Groups I, III, and IV merge to such an extent that it is perhaps preferable to regard them as the evolution of a single style, the Newcastle group being influenced by association with the Dutch and by a temporary and partial reversion to the declining styles which had their roots in Venice.

The division which it is intended to adopt here is between earlier stems of plain glass (i.e. Groups I–IV, VI, and VIII) and the twist stems and later plain glass (i.e. Groups V, VII, and IX–XII). Group XIII is universal in the period and can be treated separately. This is a division of convenience rather than chronology, although–allowing for slight variations in dating– it roughly divides the century into two; it also divides the techniques.

The earliest shape of the baluster period (Plates 51–53 and 57–60) is an inverted baluster set on a folded foot and surmounted by a bowl with straight sides – the remaining Venetian influence – and a solid base. A tear in the base of the bowl and another in the wider part of the baluster is common. This shape is evident after about 1680 and at first appears in a metal of considerable brilliance and often of a bluish cast. Almost all the very early glasses have the folded foot (see Fig. 12b), although the width of the fold varies considerably. The technique of the 'fold' was employed to create a strong edge on the foot, for the metal is inclined to be brittle. It has been suggested that a very wide fold is indicative of an English glass, but this is not an acceptable hypothesis, for some of the earliest glasses have a narrow fold and some foreigners have an excessively wide one. By 1700 the folded foot is not invariable (although still predominant), for the domed foot (see Fig. 12) appears and this may be either folded or plain. A plain foot without the dome is apparent at about the same date, but on the whole these two forms are later in the period.

The bowl at first is invariably straight-sided with a solid base as in Plate 57 (with the occasional cup-topped funnel and bucket-topped funnel appearing as chronological freaks), but by 1700 the bell-bowl is accepted (see Plate 51). Again this has the solid base–unlike the Dutch style—but it varies from an exaggerated, waisted bell to a form which is little more than conical and scarcely merits the name of bell. This is undoubtedly the forerunner of the later trumpet. The bowl was normally set straight on to the stem without any collaring, although a few early examples do show a rudimentary collar.

The stem, however, undergoes considerable changes during the period 1680–1725. The simple inverted baluster becomes by 1700 elaborated to include a wide variety of knop forms, of which the earliest is probably the angular knop and the latest the true baluster which is evident only after about 1710. The forms that may be encountered are set out below in order of frequency, starting with the most common, with the earliest date of appearance added (see Fig. 13).

Inverted Baluster 1680
Annulated Knop 1705
Angular Knop 1690
True Baluster 1710
Simple Knop 1690
Drop Knop 1690
Acorn Knop 1700
Cylinder Knop 1705
Mushroom Knop 1705
Ovoid Knop 1700
Dumb-bell Knop 1715

Of these, at least three dropped out of favour at a relatively early date and do not reappear after about 1725. The heavy angular, the ovoid, and the mushroom knop were unsuited to glasses once they lost the heaviness of appearance which marks the period prior to 1725. Of the others it must be admitted that the juxtaposition of certain forms of knop created the appearance of another form before it was made as an entity. Thus, even in 1690, the juxtaposition of two simple knops is seen as the inspiration of the dumb-bell knop, which only emerges as a definite form much later.

The baluster period merges with that of the balustroid (see plates 61–64) about 1720. The tendency towards a lighter and smaller type of glass had already begun to manifest itself by 1710, for the early single 'flint' glass had given way very quickly to double flint and the makers appear to have allowed their exuberance over a colourless metal, which could be blown thick, to run to extremes. Even the sober would find themselves straining to lift some of the larger goblets of 1700 to their lips–a 14 inch-high goblet can weigh heavily! When one speaks of a 'colourless' metal of this period it is, of course, a relative term. The early steel-blue changes during the first half of the century to green, black, and then grey, although the tints are often elusive and exceptions are fairly numerous. Yellow, pink, and brown tints are more common in foreign glasses–a white metal is late.

The bowl shape changes considerably. The solid-based straight-sided bowl is no longer fashionable, and the solid base of the bell is less noticeable, though still there (see Plate 63). The trumpet shape has come into its own and we begin to find examples of the ogee bowl from about 1725, which develops in its turn into the ovoid shape. One can also observe in some specimens the genesis of the bucket bowl; the cup shape (which is early) becomes progressively less common. Occasionally in the later part of the period there is engraving or some moulding or fluting of the bowl, but balustroid glasses as a class rely on their stem for effect.

The foot is now either folded or plain–in either event there is a fairly high conical kick (particularly noticeable in Plate 64)– with the occasional domed foot. The last category grows progressively rarer and the folded foot is predominant until about 1740.

We now continue to look at the stem. As has been mentioned above, certain knop formations died out, being basically unsuited to the smaller, lighter glasses. The inverted baluster continues in favour, but is a far less common feature than the simple knop, which appears in all degrees of compression, from the complete sphere to the almost flat disc, with layers making up annulated knops. Collars are frequent–they also served to disguise weld-marks–at the top and occasionally at the bottom of the stem. There is an air of general refinement of the earlier baluster form and–until about 1730–35–considerable origina-lity and charm. Thereafter there are a great number of glasses with simple knopping, some containing a few tears, as if the makers are anxious to turn to a new style and are merely pro-ducing this style to meet demand without enthusiasm. Of one type mention must be made, somewhat reluctantly; this is the so-called Kit-Kat type. It has been suggested, on grounds that are decidedly equivocal, that a true baluster surmounted by a trumpet bowl in a two-piece glass was a shape exclusive to a society, formed in 1703 to promote the Protestant succession, at the pastrycook's shop of one Christopher Kat in King Street, Westminster. The club was exclusive, there being only thirty members, among whom were the Duke of Marlborough and (later) Addison, Steele, and Sir Robert Walpole. In view of the limited membership and the considerable number of early ex-amples of these glasses extant, the name should long ago have been discarded, except that it has become a convenient term to describe the style. Thus is the error given new life!

From the balustroid glasses we may now turn to the form known as the light (or Newcastle) baluster (1735–65). The constant trade between the Tyne and the Netherlands clearly had some influence, for Newcastle glasses often have very large bowls–either straight-sided or bell–after the Dutch fashion, but small bowls are extremely infrequent. Many of this group were exported to Holland and were engraved there, a fact which until recently caused many perfectly good Newcastle glasses to be classified as foreigners.

The foot in the Newcastle style is either plain or folded in a neat, narrow fold. The domed foot is not common and the later plain foot predominates over the folded by about three to two. The high kick in the foot of early glasses becomes less noticeable as the period progresses.

The metal of the Newcastle glasses is of a very high standard, which is particularly creditable when one considers that the detailed knowledge of lead-metal was initially denied to the provinces, having been maintained as a closely guarded trade secret by the London glasshouses. It was both clearer and thinner than that of the earlier period, and striation of the metal is more regular and reduced. The workmanship is generally superb; for evidence of this one has only to look at Plates 69–72.

The stems of the group are perhaps best defined by reference to the tall Dutch glasses (see Plates 43–44), which were almost certainly the forerunners of this style. Knopping becomes progressively more refined and less definite, which creates hazards in classification. The inverted and true balusters are frequent, the dropknop and annulated knop less so.

Predominantly the stems are of serried simple knopping without there being any definite form of knop. Collaring exists, but is restricted in the main to the base of the bell bowl, the straight-sided and trumpet bowls more frequently being set straight onto the knopping or onto a plain section of stem of minimal length ($\frac{1}{4}$–$\frac{1}{2}$ inch). Knops with multiple tears are more common in the latter part of the period, but the single tear is evident throughout in either a baluster or swelling knop. This group is certainly the most elegant of those groups where knopping is a feature but until recently was seldom given its own category. It deserves it, for the tall refined glasses are not comparable to the squatter varieties of the balustroid type. The style was perhaps not very widely adopted, and yet, although originating in Newcastle, it was not wholly confined to that area. It is tempting, in view of the fine natural resources locally available to the glassmakers of the north-east, to suggest that those glasses of really fine material belong to Newcastle and the inferior to other centres; however, this is entirely speculation.

We must now move back in time to look at the moulded pedestal group (Plates 54–56 and 65), which Haynes dates 1715–65. In this group it is fair to say that 1715 is the earliest date possible and 1765 stretches the period to its utter limits, for the moulded pedestal stem died out some time before the Newcastle glasses. The group is generally referred to as 'Silesian', which is somewhat misleading. It is true that the style originated very soon after the Hanoverian George I came to the throne, but that is the only contemporary explanation of the title, for the Germans here either adopted, or else chanced upon, the style at a later date. The term, however, is generally accepted because of its brevity.

What commenced as a simple four-sided pedestal very soon developed into a six-sided version, and equally quickly into the eight-sided style which represents most of the period. Recalling that we have moved back into the baluster period, the reader will not be surprised to meet initially the straight-sided bowl with a solid base. Occasionally in the early period thistle-shaped bowls occur, the base of the thistle being solid. Foot patterns follow the normal trend, except that the domed foot is of longer endurance and of more general acceptance in this group than in others.

Taking the characteristics of the three classes separately, it is not difficult to see why this shape never became particularly popular for wineglasses, but lent itself admirably to *tazzas* and sweetmeat-glasses.

The four-sided pedestal is made over a very limited period – less than ten years – and relies entirely on the novel shape for effect, although a few examples have in relief at the top of the pedestal 'GOD SAVE KING GEORGE' (one word on each side), or G.R. and crowns. Collaring and knopping are absent and a domed foot is most unusual, the normal form being folded.

The six-sided pedestal, which first appears about 1720, had little more success than the four-sided, but here there can be knopping between bowl and pedestal, and the pedestal may occasionally be mounted on a series of collars. This collaring, where it appears, is almost invariably over a domed foot rather than the folded foot, which in its turn is far more usual than the plain.

The style still retains a certain classical elegance, but the shoulders of the pedestal which have hitherto for the most part been left plain – any inscription appearing on the four-sided pedestal being just below the shoulders – are now decorated or shaped in the mould much more frequently than before. The collector may expect to find wineglasses of this class more easily than the four-sided, but he may find also a sweetmeat-glass or a taperstick. If he does, he is fortunate, for they are far from common.

When the eight-sided pedestal makes its appearance in about 1725–30, the style begins to run riot. Moulding is used on foot and bowl, with the inevitable result that the glass becomes unsuitable for drinking. A true wineglass is relatively rare and sweetmeat-glasses (or any non-drinking glass) predominate; the only common form of drinking glass which one may expect to encounter is the wide-mouthed champagne glass. The reader must recall that we are still speaking of the formal moulded pedestal, for the makers of the Newcastle style also appear to have considered the style and produced a few long-stemmed wineglasses in which the moulded section is stretched and often slightly wrythen. The moulded pedestal was, however, ill suited to this adaptation and such glasses are rare, being restricted to a fairly limited period between about 1740–55.

Almost certainly this group of glasses lost favour as a result of overelaboration. By the end of their period they were wholly out of harmony with their contemporary styles in glass. The discriminating purchaser of furniture was beginning to turn from the style of Chippendale to the lighter style of Sheraton, while the builder was tiring of Palladian architecture and turning to such people as the Adam brothers for designs in a lighter vein. The purchaser of glass also sought elegance without too much solidity, and the pedestal stem was doomed. It is only to be wondered at that it should have survived so long as it did.

The plain-stemmed glasses (see Plates 66–67), which numerically constitute by far the largest group of the century, are also by far the most difficult to classify or date, common as they are from about 1725 onwards. They represent in the main the glass of the tavern or the reasonably well-to-do home and vary from the crudest to the perfect, in both design and metal, and defy attribution by style to any particular area.

The best and perhaps only guide to this group is the dating of the bowl and foot. We have already seen the early developments of bowl formation as far as the ogee bowl. The straight-sided bowl by 1740 had become the shape generally referred to as the 'round funnel'. From their very simplicity of stem we do not expect to find complex bowl formations and any shape but the simple is rare. The ovoid bowl is a late development and the trumpet bowl in all its mutations is probably the earliest and most enduring. The bucket bowl, although basically a simple shape, is rarer than might be expected and–like the ovoid bowl– belongs to a period after 1760. The cup bowl, although encountered in coloured glass occasionally, is rare in clear glass and disappeared for a time in the middle of the century. Of the complex shapes in this group the author has only encountered the Norwich, a single example of the waisted ogee, and the saucer-topped round funnel.

The only assistance to be obtained from the stem is the existence or absence of a tear. Such a feature in a completely plain stem suggests an early glass (i.e. prior to 1740), but is a far from reliable guide.

The foot of the plain-stemmed series is less influenced by current fashions than one would expect. Being made for hard wear, the folded foot continues right through the century; the domed foot, being somewhat cumbersome and vulnerable, dies a very early death, being virtually absent after 1730. Specialised foot formations (such as the oversewn, overstrung, and terraced) occur from about 1750, and the flanged and firing foot are frequent from 1740, predominantly in the smaller glasses such as drams. A moulded foot is infrequent and moulding is normally restricted to simple divisions into panels.

There now remains one group of glasses before we come to the twist stems, and it is a group which is neglected by many authors and therefore not as widely recognised as it should be; the hollow-stem group (see Plate 68) is extremely small and will appeal to those who seek rarity rather than beauty, since by virtue of their construction artistic scope is limited. Let us first define what is meant by 'hollow stem'. It is the deliberate use of a hollow cylinder as the stem, the cylinder being closed at the ends by the welding on of the bowl and foot. It is important to distinguish them from plain-stem glasses with a particularly elongated tear which involve a different structural technique. The object of this freak design is not clear, although it may have been a measure taken to reduce the tax payable under the Glass Excise Act of 1746. None the less some of the glasses in the group are not particularly light in weight. The metal used is often brittle and, since the folded foot is not usual, some are exceptionally fragile; perfect examples are scarce. Knopping is non-existent, the only practical form of stem decoration being a central swelling to give an over-all cigar shape. Bowl formations are invariably simple, being restricted to the commonest contemporary forms of the period of manufacture (at the widest, 1745–60). The rarity of this little group is not always appreciated, and since they have little artistic status they are frequently and wrongly dismissed as another form of plain stem.

They represent only a fractional percentage of eighteenth-century glass and appear on the market with diminishing frequency.

We shall see in the next chapter that just as the hollow stem appears as a freak in the stems of plain glass, so it has its contemporary equivalent among the twist stems in the incised twist. Although, strictly speaking, this type would fall into the plain glass category, it is more logical to let it take its place in the twist series. The reason for the emergence and rapid death of either style requires more explanation than research has hitherto provided.

For further reference:

See Bibliography.

CHAPTER EIGHT

The Eighteenth Century: 2

THE air-twist stem (see Plates 75–84) is a development peculiar to England. How it originated is a matter for speculation, and there are two distinct schools of thought on the subject. The more popular theory is that it developed accidentally as the result of tears that became elongated and twisted; the other, which is equally tenable, is that incised or moulded spirals on the outside of the stem became accidentally enclosed during manufacture and thus formed a crude air-twist.

As Barrington Haynes is at pains to point out, his dating represents the main period of currency, and he gives this group the dates 1745–70. There is in existence, however, one glass that must be regarded as a freak *avant-garde* development; this is shown by Grant Francis and he dates it to the end of the seventeenth century. In this specimen the air-twist is certainly not the result of a tear becoming elongated, and the spiral is sufficiently close to the surface for some rippling to be felt on the outside, a fact which perhaps lends strength to the second theory.

The earliest form of air-twist occurs in two-piece glasses where the bowl and stem are a drawn trumpet. This is not surprising when one considers the difficulties inherent in making the three-piece version, for the tidy completion of the twist under the bowl on a simple plain-shaped stem presented a problem to which no immediate solution was found. The over-all trumpet shape does not lend itself to the use of a domed foot and this feature is accordingly most infrequent, although it is not uncommon with later bell-bowl styles; plain and folded feet appear with equal frequency in the early stages. The air-twist is almost always a simple multiple-spiral (often abbreviated to M.S.A.T.) prior to 1745.

Needless to say, the makers were not for long content with the limitation in respect of bowl shapes, and they discovered that if the stem ended at the bowl with a knop (as in Plate 77), it tended to conceal the irregularity of the 'sawn-off' spiral, or to allow for normal termination as in the trumpet, and gave them freedom to use any bowl form they chose. From the examples known, which include a bell bowl, it is clear that even so they encountered some difficulty in obtaining a neat and natural ending, particularly where they tried to run the twist into the solid base of the bell in a two-piece glass (see Plate 75). The tooling under the bowl tended to close the twist, so that the part in the solid base of the bowl appears as a separate decoration.

Ultimately the attempt to take the twist into the bowl is given up, and by about 1745 we find a wide variety of bowl shapes developing in three-piece glasses, the most popular being the round funnel; less frequent are examples of the ogee and bucket. Some double or complex bowls occur, of which the most usual is the saucer-topped, although even this is rare. By now the foot is almost always plain. Once the makers have mastered the multiple-spiral we begin to find knopping more frequently, the skill with which regularity of the spiral is maintained varying considerably, and it is probable that the more knopping there is, the later the date of the glass. There was, however, a limit to the ingenuity which could be displayed with the multiple-spiral –it could be either made into bands with clear metal between, or drawn into a very tight spiral, or a very loose one, but nothing more. The double spiral (i.e. one pattern within the other) appears for the first time about 1750, the inner spiral being almost invariably tightly drawn and giving the effect of a cable, and the mixtures as before in the outer spiral. Such glasses are infrequent, for their manufacture left little scope for error and they are nearly all three-piece glasses; the stem could not be worked as a double spiral in a two-piece glass without extreme complications. Knopping is precluded.

So far we have dealt with a twist of which the cross-section is a simple circle, but there is another type which really does not fit into the general classification. This is known as a 'mercury-twist' (see Plate 78), not from any connection with mercury but because of its brilliant silvery appearance. It is difficult to date accurately, since it is confined largely to the trumpet-shaped two-piece glasses; but it is clearly a later development of the normal spiral, and the few other shapes of bowl found in conjunction with the mercury-twist are late; a fair date is about 1760. The effect is achieved by two variations. First, a metal with a high lead content is often used in an attempt to give greater brilliance; and, secondly, the cross-section of the air-twist is enlarged and in many cases flattened to create the appearance of a corkscrew. Occasionally the mercury-twist is used in conjunction with the ordinary air-twist, but it is far more pleasing on its own, an opinion apparently endorsed by the makers, for the mixed air and mercury-twist is relatively uncommon, except in a form where the mercuric nature is not emphatic.

Decoration of the air-twist series, where it occurs, is predominantly wheel-engraving. Moulded bowls and enamelling do make rare appearances, but the style has a fluid line and both forms of decoration intrude. Jacobite emblems appear frequently on glasses of this group and a fair number of other commemorative glasses are of this style. There is more inclination to formality of style in the engraving of these glasses than is evident in opaque-twist glasses, again giving the impression that the glass was an entity which required no frivolous adornment.

One form of decoration exists on the air-twist glasses which seems peculiar to this group and is only occasionally encountered. On a straight M.S.A.T. stem without knops there appears a thin superimposed belt of clear glass half-way up, giving the effect of a frill; this is often classified as a 'vermicular collar' (see Plate 75). The belt is seldom more than $\frac{1}{8}$–$\frac{1}{4}$ inch wide or high, and is normally wavy, or else two narrow straight collars. The incidence of this strange adornment is minimal and accordingly such glasses are coveted.

The opaque-twist group (1745–80) is not basically an English style, although it reached a higher standard in this country than on the Continent. We have seen earlier that the Venetians had developed the technique of introducing white canes into clear glass, and the opaque-twist represents the culmination of this glass form. Artists of the nineteenth and twentieth centuries have sought to reproduce these glasses, but their success has seldom attained the peaks surmounted by the craftsmen of the eighteenth century. The collection of this group alone can occupy those interested for the rest of their life and still be incomplete, for there are infinite variations of the twist: 158 different combinations have been noted and there must be more, occurring with a wide variety of bowls and feet.

It is impossible to do more than outline the principal constituents of the opaque-twist stem and leave the reader to work out the permutations. Basically the opaque cane introduced can be either a circular-sectioned 'thread' or a flat 'tape'. Both threads and tapes may be varying sizes and may be linked with further tapes or threads to create a broad ribbed band, or separated but parallel.

The simplest form is the multiple-spiral in which parallel canes spiral up the stem, the central part of the cross-section remaining in clear glass. This is known as a single-series twist. There may, however, be other canes spiralling concentrically within, thus leading to double-series or triple-series twists. No examples are known in which more than three series exist. By manipulation of the canes numerous effects can be created, varying from a single broad tape taken up the stem like a corkscrew to multiple-spiral threads twisted tightly to create a cable effect which may itself be straight or spiralling. The inner series of necessity will be more tightly wound than the outer series and on a triple-series twist the cable effect and the corkscrew are the most frequent for the innermost series. The most usual forms are set out below:

Multiple-spiral: all threads running in parallel spirals at the perimeter of the stem.

Corkscrew tape: either a single broad tape or two intertwined, twisted in corkscrew fashion.

Cable: closely wound threads or tapes creating a spiral rope effect.

Gauze: somewhat finer threads loosely twisted, but otherwise similar to the cable.

Lace: numerous fine tapes corkscrewing in series.

These are the basic forms and the variety already available by permutation is extensive. The makers found innumerable refinements or variations within each form and executed the work with amazingly consistent accuracy. Whether the relatively small number of inferior English twists now existing is the result of high glasshouse standards, or merely the law of survival of the best, will never be known, but it is clear that the art was generally practised to a very high standard, as in Plates 85–97.

Initially white canes appeared on their own, but when coloured canes (as in Plates 98–99) or air-twists are introduced the variations are limitless. Bearing in mind the intricacy of some of the twists, we should not expect to find knopping in any except the single-series twist glasses. A few double-series glasses have knopping, but these normally have a fairly simple twist build-up which would not be destroyed by the fashioning of a knop. Even so the result can be somewhat irregular. With the triple-series twist, which is most unusual in any event, no knopped example is known.

Bowl shapes run the full gamut, the simple ogee and the round funnel being the most common, the bucket and trumpet frequent, and the lipped or waisted varieties much less so. The double ogee, either saucer-topped, or pan-topped has always been a scarce form, and although more common in this group than in any other, it becomes progressively rarer as the period proceeds. The form of bowl known as 'Norwich' or 'Lynn' (see Plate 91) from its place of origin appears in this group. The best description of this bowl is an inverted beehive with the over-all shape of the round funnel, the ridging of the bowl varying from the definite to a mere shadow; the terraced foot (see Plate 93) sometimes called 'Norwich' is in no wise connected, and in relation to feet the word Norwich is to be eschewed.

The foot of the opaque-twist glasses is normally plain. Occasional early examples of the folded foot occur, and though unusual, they are far more common than the domed foot, of which the incidence is extremely limited. The specialised foot forms appear in this group more than in any other–the firing, terraced, oversewn, and overstrung being not uncommon, particularly in the drams and shorter glasses. A flanged foot on a glass of this group has never been seen by the author, but it is a form more remarkable by its absence than it would be by its presence.

During the periods of the air-twist and opaque-twist there are two compromise styles, the first normally called the 'Composite' stem. These are the glasses in which a clear metal section is combined with either an air-twist or an opaque-twist to form the stem, and they frequently bear some over-all resemblance to the Newcastle glasses. The twist section is normally a simple multiple-spiral, from which one is tempted to set them in the

early part of the period given by Haynes (1745–75). A few
glasses with a double-series twist are almost certainly of the later
part. The clear glass section, which may be little more than a
clear knop, may appear either above or below the twist section,
the union being always represented by a knop in one or other
section. Air-twist sections outnumber opaque by a very large
margin and the known colour-twist examples can be counted on
the fingers.

Bowl formations are limited to the bell, trumpet, and round
funnel, and the foot is plain with occasional domes. Only one
folded example has been seen and that on a very inferior glass.
These glasses are rarer than might be expected from the length
of their period of currency and the variety of possible forms.

In the previous chapter we observed an odd and very small
group with hollow stems. The second compromise style among
the twist glasses coincides in time with the hollow-stem glasses,
but can scarcely have been the result of the Excise Act. Perhaps
the incised twist (see Plates 73–74) was the poor man's version
of the air-twist, but from the small number extant it is clear that
the style never found great favour. They have, however, received
far more attention than the hollow-stem group, despite the fact
that they are seldom beautiful and rarely of a high standard of
craftsmanship. We have already seen that possibly the technique
was known much earlier, but the glasses of 1750 are on the whole
crudely incised, becoming somewhat more refined during the ten
or fifteen years of the period. Knopping is extremely scarce,
representing perhaps 3 or 4 per cent of a class which is itself
scarce. Bowl forms are restricted to the simple forms and may
occasionally be lightly moulded as in Plate 74. The foot is, so
far as known examples go, almost always plain, the incidence of
the folded foot amounting to only a small percentage of the
group. As with the hollow stems, the metal is inclined to be
brittle.

Some authorities, among them Hartshorne and Grant
Francis, put all the glasses of this series to a very much earlier
date than Haynes, but this is the result of reviewing them in the
light of metal. Admittedly the metal appears early, for it lacks
the refinement current in the middle of the century, but this can
indicate the product of a backward glasshouse as much as an
early date; if the reader accepts that this was the poor man's

version of the air-twist, we should not expect to find it in the finest metal of the period. If the glasses really belong to the early period, one would expect more examples of the folded foot and predominantly early bowl forms. The disciples of the earlier dating must also explain away late bowl shapes and the very few examples of engraving, all of which are in styles more in accord with the period set by Haynes. The normal suggestion, that the engraving was added at a later date, is not to be favoured, for none of the three engraved examples so far encountered have had engraving of any particular significance, or really merited the attention of the engraver at a time when there were available other varieties of glass of far greater contemporary appeal.

The faceted stem (see Plate 106) became fashionable in England in the 1750's, by which time the technique was well known and had been widely practised in Bohemia for many years. From fairly modest beginnings the style grew more and more to rival the opaque-twist, until in 1777 a tax was set on enamel glass which included the opaque-twist stems. Thereafter faceting was predominant, and it is not easy to set a final date on the period; for we are now approaching the golden era of cutting and the style merges almost unnoticeably into the Regency and Victorian styles.

Let us look, however, at the characteristics of those that are undoubtedly eighteenth-century glasses. The bowl shape is always simple, the ovoid being particularly popular, with the round funnel and an indeterminate ogee only a little behind in favour. Only one complex bowl shape has been encountered, a waisted ogee of extreme ugliness, and even lipping is little used. The limiting factor in regard to bowl shapes is the convention– one may call it that, for it appears to be universal–that the faceting shall continue on to the base of the bowl. Quite clearly this eliminates those shapes which widen from the stem at an angle of anything like ninety degrees.

The feet of this group are of particular interest, partly for their variety and partly because of their assistance in dating. The latter point is important, for the collector will occasionally encounter a plain-stem glass which has subsequently been cut, the glass thus masquerading out of its true period. In the case of a glass with a folded foot this is almost certainly what has happened. Another guide which may sometimes reveal an earlier glass is the presence of the rough pontil mark, which was generally polished off in this group; this, however, is not an infallible test. The final guidance which the foot may give is its basically unsuitable shape for cutting in conjunction with the stem. In some facet-cut glasses one can see that the whole was made without any thought of cutting, and the cutting ends in an untidy mess at the bottom of the stem.

The plain foot predominates, although it may be as thick as a firing foot in order to take cutting (or occasionally moulding), but the cut foot is not common except where the bowl has received more than the usual share of the cutter's attention; i.e. with a plain bowl one would normally expect a plain foot. The domed foot makes rather a come-back in the period and is not now so rarely encountered as some authorities in the past have found. That is not to say that it is common; but a reasonable number of examples are to be found, on which the cutting was certainly done at the time of manufacture. No dome without cutting has been encountered by this writer.

The cutting of the plain foot varies immensely, the form being determined in part by the thickness of the foot. Radial cutting is most frequent, although on the whole a late characteristic, while the scalloped edge of a thick foot is uncommon and also early. Cutting on the underside of the foot is a later development, and one which from about 1780 to the present day has endured in favour.

Thus far we have progressed without defining faceting. Two forms are common, the simple four-sided diamond shape and the hexagonal. Any other form purporting to be of the eighteenth century should be viewed with circumspection, both as to date and nationality, for Continental glasses frequently have faceting built up of more than one shape, rather than diamond or hexagon over-all. The faceting generally rises to the shoulder of the bowl from the angle of the foot, although in some instances the entire bowl is faceted. Simple knopping, over which the cutting may continue in regular, elongated facets, is fairly frequent, but always at the top or centre of the stem. A prolonged search for a glass having a knop at the base of the faceted stem has proved fruitless.

Decoration of the bowls of this group apart from cutting is common. Almost all is wheel-engraving, and much of the engraving is enhanced by the polishing of certain engraved part to create highlights. This in itself was not a new technique, but one which achieved its zenith during the period of the faceted stem. The commonest examples are those having a formal engraved border below the rim of the bowl. Floral, pictorial, and occasionally Jacobite subjects are not unusual, although the last are to be considered with care; cutting disguises metal colour to a certain extent and among the styles of the later part of the eighteenth century this group represents the most simply reproduced.

We have now seen the predominant stem forms of the century and the associated characteristics of each group. Before turning to the less distinctive glasses of the period which fall into no clear category, let us look at some of the decorative techniques and the artists who employed them.

Of the eighteenth-century English engravers none is known whose works can be recognised, but the standards achieved suggest that many had experience in fields of engraving other than glass. Under a microscope one can sometimes detect a technique characteristic of the silver engraver used for the performance of a particular intricacy, and it is probable that there was some liaison between the glassmakers and the silversmiths through the freelance engravers; the reader will recall that in an earlier period Anthony de Lysle engraved on pewter, as well as for Verzelini.

Having mentioned the microscope, it is worth pointing out that time spent comparing engraving under any powerful form of magnification is well spent; different techniques, different equipment, and different grinding speeds all show variations indiscernible by the naked eye. The value of this is particularly noticeable in regard to Jacobite and other commemorative glass.

Diamond-point stipple engraving is not a technique much practised in England in the eighteenth century and accordingly examples are exceptionally rare. The art was perfected in Holland and appears on exported Newcastle balusters. On glasses of three other groups, the opaque-twist, the plain stem and the faceted stem, isolated examples are known; these, too, were possibly Dutch work, although the glass is in each case English.

Etching, a development of the acid-embossing introduced in Germany by Schwanhardt, was not adopted as a decorative form until after 1800. Any previous example must be regarded as experimental.

In the field of enamelling the eighteenth century produced a few really successful artists. Michael Edkins (1734–1811) is primarily noted for his enamelling of opaque and coloured glass in Bristol; but, in view of the wide range of articles that he enamelled (which we know from his business ledgers), it appears that he also worked on a certain amount of clear 'flint' glass. Irish enamelled glass of the last decades of the century is often attributed to one James Donovan, who certainly enamelled pottery and also owned a glasshouse just outside Dublin, but there is no solid evidence to support the attribution. William Absalon of Great Yarmouth also enamelled glass towards the end of the century, the greater number of pieces being coloured or opaque; but signed examples on clear glass do exist, although for the main part these are cheap mementoes of Yarmouth. That other enamellers were at work is an inevitable conclusion, but only a few are known to us by name.

The best known of the enamellers, and deservedly so, were the Beilby family of Newcastle, whose earliest known work dates from 1762. Their superiority in the field is not only due to their artistic talent, but also to the quality of the enamel. Although the greater part of their work is in simple white enamel of a rather less milk-and-water white than that of their foreign contemporaries, they excelled in the enamelling of armorial glasses executed in full colour, and in white enamels in which a little colour is used to pick out or emphasise some feature. Subject-matter varies widely from landscape to birds, grapes, and flowers. Signed works, which are sufficiently few to command high prices, have the signature 'Beilby', 'Beilby inv. & pinx.', or in one case 'Beilby Junr Ncastle Invt & Pinxt'. Normally it is impossible to tell which member of the family is responsible.

William Beilby senior (1706–65) was a jeweller and silversmith. Married in 1733, he had seven children, of whom two, William born in 1740 and Mary born in 1749, took up glass-enamelling. In 1760 the family moved to Newcastle and the business of glass-enamelling flourished. The perfection of some of the armorial glasses may be due in part to the heraldic knowledge of a brother Ralph, who was three years younger than William junior, but already widely known for his carving and engraving of coats of arms in wood. In 1772 Mary became invalid and may not be responsible for the later glasses. She was then only twenty-three and it is probable that only a small percentage of Beilby glasses are, in fact, attributable to Mary; it is often suggested that she specialised in the floral designs such as Plate 96. In 1778 their mother died, and William and Mary left Newcastle, after which little is known of them and still less of their enamelling.

The period of the Beilby family is relatively short, and since most of their early glasses were armorial it is dangerous to attribute to them glasses manufactured much before 1760, for most of their enamelling dates to the ten years following and would presumably be executed on reasonably new glass. There are grounds for believing that the armorial glasses were specially made for the purpose, since the shape is extremely rare in the proportions shown in Plate 97. It is not uncommon for the first-class engravers today to have glass made for the purpose, and the clients for whom the Beilby family enamelled armorial works were well able to bear the expense of a specially made glass.

Before turning to the largest group of glasses, those having only rudimentary stems, it is essential to classify the various shapes according to use. Complications arise because, then as now, certain glasses were used for more than one purpose, but in most cases the intended use can be defined. The terminology used below is given as general guidance, but is not universally accepted. The basic shape used for comparison is the wineglass.

ALE

The ale of the eighteenth century being stronger than today's brew, the capacity of these glasses is normally less than ⅓ pint – the bowl being about 4 inches high, although both dwarf and giant examples occur. The 'ale' appears in all stem groups, being rarest in the balusters. This rareness may be due to failure in recognition, for engraving was not practised in the very early part of the eighteenth century and the familiar hops and barley motif is absent. In the later major groups such engraving is common, but faceted-stem ale-glasses are not frequent and engraved examples rarer still. The engraving is normally two barley ears with stalks crossed on one side of the glass and a hop bloom with a leaf on either side on the reverse. The rarest known engraving is two ears of barley set sideways uncrossed and alone. Other rarities include: (*a*) two hop blooms hanging from two barley stalks, (*b*) one leaf only to the hop bloom, and (*c*) four ears of barley without hops. Enamelled motifs are exceptional and normally of the Beilby period.

In addition to the main stem groups there are innumerable ale-glasses with no stem or a rudimentary knop between foot and V-bowl; most of these are dwarf ales. The dating of these is perilous, but certain features are early. A knop pinched to create four projections is probably pre-1700. Gadrooning, the creation of a fine spiral swirling on the bowl, seems to have started about 1720 and remained popular into the nineteenth century, while a glass wrythen to the top of the bowl is more characteristic of the first half of the eighteenth century. Some guidance can be obtained from the foot shape, but essentially the styles are universal to the period. Giant ales, similar to modern lager-glasses, but longer and sometimes called 'half-yards', are encountered from about 1740.

BOOT OR BUTE

A drinking glass shaped like a boot. See Plate 103. These were allegedly made as a gibe at the Earl of Bute, the unpopular Prime Minister, but their frequency among the glasses of Liège and Antwerp suggests that this is incorrect. Varying sizes up to 15 inches have been seen, the smaller specimens (i.e. under $3\frac{1}{2}$ inches) being less common than those between $3\frac{1}{2}$ inches and 8 inches.

CHAMPAGNE

The drink was introduced to England in the late seventeenth century and glasses specifically for this wine do not seem to have been made before about 1725, when they begin to appear in the moulded pedestal and light baluster groups. The shape is controversial, since the bowl, shallow as in modern champagnes, is similar to that used in sweetmeat- or sucket-glasses; the only distinguishing mark must be the practicability of drinking from the particular glass. After the initial abundance of champagnes, the makers produced singularly few, and those in the later groups are rare.

COACHING GLASS

A glass having no foot below the stem. Since it could not be set down while any of the contents remained, drinking when the coaches stopped was not unduly prolonged. Not in evidence prior to 1775.

CORDIAL

An extremely small bowl set on a stem of normal proportions for a wine. Cordials were the lady's drink of the middle part of the century and approximated to a weak modern liqueur. From about 1730.

DECEPTIVE GLASS

See *Toastmaster*.

DRAM

Also known as a 'gin' or 'Hogarth' from the glasses depicted in his series *The Rake's Progress* and elsewhere. A normal wine-sized bowl set on a short stout stem, the whole being about 3–4 inches high. Drams also exist without a stem, but are then confused with the small tumbler. 'Dram' is a Scots term and the thistle-shaped bowl is not infrequent. From about 1725.

DWARF ALE

See *Ale*.

FIRING GLASS

Similar to a dram, but having a very strong heavy foot up to $\frac{1}{4}$ inch thick which could be rapped on the table without damage. The rapping of a number of such glasses produces a sound like volleys of gunfire. These glasses occur mainly in the plain, air-twist and opaque-twist groups and date from about 1730 to 1770; all are heavily made glasses and many bear masonic emblems. Despite their rough usage they are frequent, the solid foot being more common than the flanged (Plate 100).

FLUTE

This very early shape (see Plate 47) was possibly used for ale, but no definite evidence is available. It does not appear to have been popular in the eighteenth century, its artistic merit being outweighed by its impractical nature. True examples are rare, but certain stemless ale-glasses might be classified as flutes.

GOBLET

The term is loosely applied to any giant drinking glass with a stem. Examples up to 17 inches high are known. It occurs mainly early and in the baluster period (although certain Newcastle glasses might fall within the category), or else in the very late eighteenth or early nineteenth century.

HALF-YARD

See *Ale*.

HOGARTH

See *Dram*.

JELLY GLASS

This class, which extends from 1690 onwards, is composed predominantly of waisted bowls or the duplex shapes such as double ogee or pan-topped bowls with or without a handle or handles and with only a rudimentary or no stem set on a domed or conical foot. Folded feet are unusual; cut and moulded examples are frequent. The comparative frequency of the double bowls in this class is referable to the popularity of syllabub, a drink made from milk, fruit, and wine or ale, and whipped to a froth, then topped with cream which ideally filled the top section of the bowl. Jellies and custards were also served in this type of glass, despite the relatively awkward shape. The primary use can often be discerned by reference to the rim, which may prohibit drinking in comfort and suggest that the contents were to be spooned out.

MONTEITH

The description is widely used to describe glasses which fit in no clear category. The origin of the name is dubious and its application too general. The word first appears in the latter part of the eighteenth century and seems to apply to small bowls, either with or without feet, which might be used for drinks or for sweetmeats and nuts, although recently it has been widely used for vessels holding four or five pints which would equally correctly be called punch-bowls. Some say that a scalloped edge is the essential detail, others that a double bowl such as the pan-top is the true Monteith. Until the true source of the description is discovered, the collector will have to regard the designation with suspicion.

PATCHSTAND

A miniature *tazza* (q.v) in most cases 3–4 inches high appearing in all stem groups and not very common. A few specialist collections exist and most examples are of fine workmanship, since they were intended as showpieces on a lady's dressing table.

POSSET POT

Similar to a modern teapot in its later stages, this shape dates back to the seventeenth century and was used for a then popular drink made from hot milk and spiced wine. The early pieces of this shape are normally a deep bowl set direct on to the foot with a cover and teapot-like spout. Handles are normal on either side. The drink ceased to be fashionable fairly early in the eighteenth century and all such vessels are rare. It has also been suggested that they were used for feeding babies, but neither reliable documentation nor any illustration of this use has been found.

RATAFIA

A tall, very narrow conical bowl of small capacity. Heights are various but generally the bowl is set on a stem normal for a wineglass of the period. Ratafia, which first appears as a drink in the very early years of the eighteenth century, is a fruit cordial and its popularity continued until about 1780. Examples are found in all groups, although faceted specimens have not been encountered, and all are difficult to obtain. The attractive shape and limited number which appear to have been produced make these glasses a valuable addition to a collection. Decoration is generally delicate and engraving or enamelling formal, befitting a glass designed for ladies (Plate 87).

RUMMER

A later and shorter-stemmed version of the goblet. The derivation from the *Römer* is obscure, but generally accepted, as being preferable to the association with rum. It was common from 1780 onwards, the heyday of this shape occurring about 1820.

STIRRUP GLASS

See *Coaching Glass*.

SWEETMEAT

Almost indistinguishable from champagnes, but some glasses (e.g. those with scalloped edges) from which it would be impossible to drink fall into this category. Dating as for champagnes.

SYLLABUB

See *Jelly Glass*.

TANKARD

Similar to the modern concept and in use in the seventeenth century. Infrequent, although the evidence suggests that they were a normal form throughout the eighteenth century. Exceptionally difficult to date by style, so the quality of the metal is perhaps the best guide.

TAZZA

A flat dish mounted on a stem that was designed principally to hold jelly glasses. From about 1710 onwards, and including many Silesian (moulded-stem) examples. Baluster-stem examples continue after the normal dating until cut stems replace them. Twist-stems are extremely rare except in the miniature examples.

TOASTING GLASS

A drinking glass with a plain, exceptionally thin stem (certainly no thicker than a pencil) which could be snapped between the fingers after drinking. All known examples are drawn trumpet bowls and the fragility of these glasses makes them most uncommon. From about 1730 onwards, but – being of consistent design – no definite dating is possible. Height is normally *c*. 9 inches.

TOASTMASTER GLASS

A cordial or dram, with exceptionally thick walls, reducing the capacity while maintaining a normal appearance. When filled many of these glasses appear to be holding a normal measure, since the walls taper towards the rim, presenting a normal surface area (Plate 101).

TODDY LIFTER

A pipette shaped like a miniature decanter. Used to lift wine from a bowl to the glass; they contain on average 2–3 ounces, enough to fill a wineglass of the period. From 1720 onwards, and for no apparent reason more common in the north than the south. Frequent from 1750 (Plate 105).

TUMBLER

Probably originating from the beaker that would not stand upright, the tumbler occurs in various forms throughout the eighteenth century, beginning with a high kick in the base and becoming gradually heavier and more solidly based. Early examples are frequently wrythen.

WAITER

See *Tazza*.

WINE

The basic shape of the all-purpose glass. Contents, generally 2–3 ounces (i.e. much less than the modern wineglass and more akin to a sherry-glass).

WINE-COOLER

A straight-sided bowl with two pouring lips diametrically opposite each other. Normally about 4 inches across and about 5 inches high. The use of this vessel is a matter of controversy, for some say that it was used to air wines to be drunk at room temperature, while others contend that it was filled with water and used either as a fingerbowl or to rinse wineglasses before a change of wine. The presence of the lips suggests that it may have been used to support punch ladles or toddy lifters, but this is purely speculation. It is perhaps preferable to regard this shape as an all-purpose vessel until positive evidence is found of a particular use.

YARD OF ALE

Similar to a coaching horn in shape, with a sphere at what would be the mouthpiece end. These glasses are still made today for a test of drinking ability, the sphere shape causing a final rush of ale when the glass is lifted above the horizontal. Made from about 1760 onwards, they are difficult to date and most examples encountered belong to the nineteenth century.

Having categorised the predominant shapes of the eighteenth-century drinking glasses and accessories, the reader is faced with the problem of dating those glasses with either no stem or a rudimentary stem. This group defies the general rules and most examples should be dated towards the end of the eighteenth or the first part of the nineteenth century, unless some particular feature points to an earlier period. It is not the intention of this book to seek to classify these glasses, although this has been attempted by previous authors, nor do illustrations appear, since they can in many cases give false impressions. There is no logical sequence either in foot or bowl form, provenance is universal, and quality infinitely varied. They provide a treacherous allure for the beginner, and, until metal recognition is instinctive, any piece should be collected for its aesthetic quality rather than as a dated item. Such advice may be condemned as dodging the issue, but the most experienced collectors are on the whole the least willing to attempt dating of such glasses by any other criterion than instinct, which cannot be translated into writing. Barrington Haynes and Francis Buckley have perhaps come nearest to a reasonable dating system, but neither claims success; and the collector of these glasses will gain more guidance from his own experience than from adherence to existing classifications.

For further reference:

See Bibliography.

CHAPTER NINE

English Commemorative Glass

THE custom of engraving glass to commemorate occasions, people, or causes was well established in England by the eighteenth century. The Verzelini goblets, the Exeter Flute, and a few other examples exist from the preceding centuries; but in the eighteenth century, with the advent of wheel-engraving, the practice became widespread, and specialist collections are now a practical proposition. Certain classes obviously have a greater attraction, but they are not necessarily the rarest. Of all the classes the Jacobite series are undoubtedly the most popular.

The decoration of the Jacobite glasses is in most cases symbolic, and in order that their significance may be understood some knowledge of the history of the Movement is desirable. The summary which follows is offered not as a complete account but as one which explains why certain forms of decoration appear on the glasses.

Charles II returned to England on 29 May 1660, a day subsequently called Oak-apple Day to commemorate the fact that after the Battle of Worcester in 1651 he was compelled to hide in an oak tree. He brought with him his brother James, Duke of York, who in the December of that year revealed that he had married Anne Hyde, a daughter of Lord Clarendon, a few months earlier. Anne Hyde gave James two children, Mary and Anne, before she died in 1671.

In 1672 James published the fact that he had been converted to Roman Catholicism, a conversion viewed with disapproval by his brother, Parliament, and the populace. His marriage, in 1673, to the Catholic Mary of Modena led to the Whigs planning to exclude him from the succession, and to his universal unpopularity. He discreetly withdrew to Brussels when things became too hot for him and on his return he took the post of Lord High Commissioner for Scotland, in which office he escaped the disfavour of the English, but incurred that of many Scots. His acquiescence in Charles's policy and his agreement to the marriage of his daughter Mary to the Protestant William of Orange, against her wishes, appeased no one – as a politician of any sort he was hopelessly inept.

When James ascended the throne in 1685 (his brother having no legitimate son) the country backed him until his Catholicism and his overt favouring of Catholics led the Protestant nobles to approach William of Orange, with a view to him replacing James. On 10 June 1688, Mary of Modena gave birth to a son and heir apparent, James Francis Edward Stuart, and the invitation to William became definite as soon as the Protestants saw a continuation of the Catholic line. Innumerable stories were circulated that the child was suppositious, but his classical Stuart looks in later life disproved them entirely. William landed in England on 5 November 1688, and James with his infant son retired to France where he died at St Germain in 1701. William himself died in 1702, being succeeded by Anne who died without a surviving child. The line of succession then passed to the Hanoverian George I.

James Francis Edward Stuart (the Old Pretender) was then thirteen, and in the eyes of many he was the rightful heir to the English throne, being the only surviving son of James II. Louis XIV immediately proclaimed him James III, and in 1708 James went to Scotland, where he expected the strongest support; but having reached the Firth of Forth he found that his communications had gone wrong and the expedition returned to France. In the September of 1715 the Earl of Mar raised his standard proclaiming James, Chevalier of St George, King of England. This was timed to coincide with a rising in Cumberland, under a Mr Forster, and a landing in the West Country by the Duke of Ormonde's troops, but Ormonde never landed; and by November, after one indecisive battle, the rebellion collapsed. James arrived in December, but on the approach of the Duke of Argyll with an army he sensibly retired to France. The French backing, half promised by Louis XIV, had been minimised by the anxiety of the Duke of Orleans, Regent for the new King Louis XV, to maintain amicable relations with England, and 'Bobbing John' Mar was too indecisive a leader for a rebellion.

In 1718 James married Maria Clementina Sobieski, a grand-daughter of King John Sobieski of Poland, by whom he had two sons, Charles Edward and Henry Benedict. She died in 1735 and James gradually lost all political aspirations and concerned himself more and more with religion. He died in Rome in 1766.

Henry had little interest in politics and devoted his life to religious study, becoming a cardinal in 1747, so he had no significant place in the Jacobite Movement's history. Charles, however, as the Young Pretender, was much more fitted for a hero's part than his father, being relatively handsome and more determined to reclaim his rightful crown. He landed at Moidart in July 1745 with only seven men, but the clans soon rallied to him and he marched south.

General Cope was sent to oppose him, but took the wrong route (and thus incidentally gave us the derisive Jacobite song, 'Hey, Johnny Cope, are you marching yet?'), so Charles was given the chance to meet up with Lord George Murray, a competent but perhaps too cautious soldier. Together they met Cope and, attacking him by surprise, achieved a bloodless victory in under half an hour at Prestonpans. General Wade, whom a worried Government sent north with a large army, marched too far to the east and missed Charles, who came south through Carlisle and Manchester as far as Derby. The support which Charles had been led to expect in England was not forthcoming, and, having once been persuaded by Murray to retreat, he found his army rapidly diminishing. The Duke of Cumberland, his next adversary, having coached north from London to Edinburgh in six days to take command of a large and well-drilled force, met a body of hungry and dispirited troops in Culloden in January 1746; his overwhelming victory earned him the name of 'The Butcher' or 'Sweet William', according to one's loyalties. Charles himself escaped by boat to Skye, through the assistance of Flora Macdonald, and subsequently to France. He returned incognito to England in 1752 and is supposed to have made a declaration of Protestantism, but his subsequent history is of little interest, his death occurring in 1788.

The principal reason for the failure of the 1745 rebellion was that Charles believed himself to have very much more support both on the Continent and in England than he in fact had. If he had gone on from Derby, the consequences are a matter of speculation, for loyalties in London were divided, but it is difficult to assess just how real his backing was farther south.

Certainly the Hanoverians were not popular, but it is probable that many of those who professed loyalty to the Jacobite line were attracted by the idea of a 'King over the water' whose cause justified secret societies. The romantics of eighteenth-century England could have no better excuse for a drinking club than this, and certainly few had any intention of becoming involved in fighting. To this general statement one must, of course, make exceptions, the best known but not necessarily the most important of these being the 'Cycle Club' or, to use its full title, 'The Cycle of The White Rose', which was founded in 1710 and endured long after Culloden. The club was based on Wrexham and it is in the north-west and Wales that the Jacobites undoubtedly had the greatest support outside Scotland. London, as one would expect, had its full share of Jacobite clubs, where the titles of Tory and Jacobite were almost interchangeable, and it is reasonable to suggest that many of the allegedly Tory clubs had strong Jacobite leanings. The Oak Society, which met at the *Crown and Anchor* in the Strand, was without doubt Jacobite, but the mystery surrounding it does nothing to authenticate certain claims regarding its glass.

Christopher Layer, a barrister who headed a conspiracy in 1722 to seize the King and Prince of Wales and bring back the Pretender, was a member of the Beaufort Club, but the club appears then to be more anti-Hanoverian than pro-Stuart, although it later became overtly Jacobite. Again secrecy has denied us any evidence as to the intentions of the club.

Many authorities regard the Society of Sea Serjeants of South Wales as a Jacobite Club, but there is no evidence to support this apart from the allegations made by Whigs when its Tory president stood for Parliament in 1754. Most of the documentary evidence, including the form of examination of candidates for admission, suggests that the society was not of a treasonable nature. The badge of this society was a dolphin and there may be some confusion with a society known as the Sons of the Dolphin, whose political proclivities are unknown.

Hunts and race-meetings were ever the scene of political dissent, and in the latter part of the century there were a considerable number of fervent Jacobite hunts, of which the best known are the Friendly and the Confederate. Lichfield Races are reputed to have been little better than a Jacobite rally.

There were many ways in which the Jacobite toast might be drunk, the commonest being to hold the wineglass over a bowl of water and to drink to the King, signifying the King over the water and not the Hanoverian impostor. Another was to drink to 'The Steward of the Realm', the twist here being that the Stuarts were Stewards of the Kingdom of Scotland long before they became kings. Naturally each club had its own particular toast, generally far more treasonable than either of the above, which were comfortably ambiguous; and some had the glasses engraved by the itinerants who were prepared to use their skill in secret. There is little doubt that many Jacobite glasses are the work of the same few engravers. The glasses peculiar to the Jacobite cause can be divided roughly into five classes.

MASONIC GLASSES

Certain masonic lodges were definitely pro-Jacobite, although of necessity these were limited in view of the Pope's condemnation of Freemasonry in 1738, which left only those lodges composed of Protestant Jacobites. Just which lodges these were is uncertain, but some of their emblems are very similar to the more commonly accepted Jacobite symbols.

COIN GLASSES

Glasses having a coin of Charles II, or James II, in the stem are now generally regarded as Jacobite, but to this there must be a limitation. The insertion of contemporary coins is a custom still carried on today, and it is only in cases where the glass is clearly eighteenth century and the coin seventeenth century that any significance should be attached. The popularity of these glasses was understandable; they in no way compromised the owner and they have an intrinsic fascination. It is clear that coins of Charles II were preferred to those of James II; James's appeal was not so universal as that of his brother, whose romantic escapades in the Civil War endeared him to those who favoured the Stuart cause. The glasses are either balusters or knopped air-twists, and the series runs from about 1715 to 1760.

'AMEN' GLASSES

The 'Amen' glasses were blatantly treasonable. Invariably of simple design (a two-piece glass with a drawn trumpet bowl and usually a tear in the stem), they were engraved in diamond-point with scrollwork, ciphers, and the Jacobite anthem, which is set out below in full, although not all the verses necessarily appear on one glass.

> God save the King I pray
> God bless the King I pray
> God save the King
> Send him Victorious
> Happy and Glorious
> Soon to reign over us
> God save the King.

> God bless the Prince of Wales
> The true born Prince of Wales
> Sent us by thee
> Grant us one favour more
> The King for to restore
> As thou hast done before the family.

> God save the Church I pray
> and Bless the Church I pray
> Pure to remain
> Against all Heresy
> and Whigs' hypocrisy
> Who strive maliciously
> Her to defame.

> God bless the Subjects all
> and save both great and small
> In every station
> That will bring home the King
> Who hath best right to reign
> It is the only thing
> Can save the nation.
>   Amen.

Less than twenty of these glasses exist and they have always proved a temptation to forgers. They are of particular interest for the variations between them. Thus in some the first verse reads 'Long to reign over us', whereas in others it reads 'Soon to reign over us' – which strengthens the treasonable significance. The second verse deals with the subject of the birth of the Young Pretender. This must refer to Charles Edward for in Jacobite eyes the 'Old Pretender' became James III before there was an organised Jacobite movement. Charles was 'true born' Prince of Wales, whereas the future George II was not. Spelling and punctuation on the glasses vary immensely, and the above version is given in modern spelling rather than any of the variations. The word 'bless' is spelt 'bliss' on all known glasses in the Scots manner, but otherwise spelling is free. The royal ciphers JIII and JVIII are general; one forgery even carries a dedication to Henry Benedict, dated 1749 – rather too late to be of any avail, since Henry had been a cardinal for two years! The standard of engraving is on the whole fairly high, although the limitations of diamond-point are evident in the tendency for the engraving to be slightly out of true. The glasses are difficult to date precisely. In books the anthem first appears in full about 1725 (see Plate 116).

SYMBOLIC GLASSES

We now come to the fourth and most complex class of Jacobite glasses, the symbolic disguised variety, which are by far the most common, since the treasonable nature of them is even now far from clear. Almost all the glasses falling within this class are engraved by the wheel, and the standard of engraving varies from the superb to the very crude. For the sake of clarity each emblem employed is treated separately.

The Rose

This, the most frequent emblem of all, has been for years and is still a much-debated subject. In its basic forms it is made up of one flower and one or two buds. Occasionally (three instances are known) there is a third bud, and more frequently, but still very rarely, a bud is empty. Before discussing the Jacobite significance attached to this form of decoration, it is as well to make it clear that the rose has been a national emblem of

Scotland since about 1350 and of England since 1485. It is in addition the symbol of secrecy, from the circumstance of the Pope's presenting consecrated roses, which were set over the confessionals in Rome in 1526 – whence the phrase *sub rosa* – so that it has been adopted over the years by many secret societies as a part of their badge. Accordingly one should not totally rule out the possibility that some glasses bearing an engraved rose have no connection with the Jacobite cause.

That the White Rose – and it must be white – was a Jacobite emblem has been proved beyond all reasonable doubt, but whether its significance was limited to James, the Old Pretender, or should be attached to the House of Stuart in general is not clear. Certainly the wearing of a white rose on 10 June, James's birthday, was an act little short of sedition, which in 1721 led to the troops in Edinburgh being ordered to remove the offending badge from the wearers. Little evidence can be found to support the theory that the white rose as an emblem of legitimacy was adopted initially by James; protestations about the circumstances of his birth would surely not run to the adoption of the badge for this reason. It is preferable to regard it as a family badge.

Before Captain Horridge expounded the most realistic theory as to the significance of the rose, it was generally held that the flower represented the Old Pretender and the buds represented his two sons. This created problems, for some early glasses have only one bud even after Henry's birth; glasses with two buds exist of the period after Henry had become a cardinal and ceased to figure in politics, and some late glasses with the flower and one bud were made when James was already dead.

Horridge, however, advanced the theory that the flower represented the English Crown, and the buds James and Charles. This is far more tenable, but his theory that the dexter bud stood for Charles and the sinister for James is perhaps taking things too far, since the sinister bud still appears after James's death in 1766. We can accept Horridge's view that Henry did not feature, except in the instances where a third bud appears. This theory avoids the difficulties of the old version and is universally applicable. Captain Horridge's view that Charles assumed the major role even before 1745 is often disputed, but if one considers the history of James after his wife's death, it certainly becomes more acceptable, the most active period of Jacobitism being from about 1738 to 1750.

There remains one major problem, which concerns a very small group of glasses in which the bud is empty. The flower is not always the simple five- or six-petal rose, but can be multi-petalled, with the dexter bud always affected. With some hesitation it is suggested that such glasses date prior to 1745, a period in which the cause awaited the nomination of a leader for the '45 rebellion, with the empty bud representing the cause awaiting fulfilment. This would also perhaps explain those glasses with two buds, one of them severed (i.e. James is considered to have lost regal aspiration). The problem remains entirely open to speculation.

It has been suggested that certain faceted-stem glasses are Jacobite even though they may have no symbols. These are glasses in which the drinker looking into the bowl sees at the base of it the rose created by the faceting on the exterior. This theory is only acceptable in a very limited number of cases where the external appearance of the cutting is subordinated to the perfection of the rose seen through the bowl. No definite evidence can be found in support of this idea and the temptation to discard it is strong.

The Thistle

This emblem is shown growing from the same stem as the rose, as well as separately, and therefore gives strength to Horridge's basic theory that the rose stood for the English Crown. The thistle clearly represents the Crown of Scotland, and since this represents a lesser and more easily attainable target it appears far less frequently; it was also, of course, a Stuart badge. It is a fairly late emblem.

The Star

Although this is generally considered to be relevant to the birth of Charles, it appears more regularly on glasses after 1740 and may well signify the guiding light of the movement. It is noted in *Customs of Scotland* (1829) that it was usual to kiss the star on one's glass when drinking the Jacobite toasts, an act more easily reconciled with the guiding-light theory than with some attribute of Charles's birth. Why not kiss the relevant bud, since that is almost invariably concomitant?

The Oak Leaf

This was the clan badge of the Stuarts, and the oak has special significance since Charles II's escapade in the Boscobel oak. The entire oak tree appears occasionally, with or without a figure in it, and such glasses are certainly connected with loyalty to the Stuart kings, even if they do not represent active Jacobitism. The greater number of glasses bearing either the leaf or tree have other Jacobite insignia. Horridge considered it a reference to Charles Edward as a grown man, but such a theory is superfluous. In any event it appears in the early 1730's.

The Blackbird

This should not be related to the snipe-like bird which is found on many masonic glasses, the significance of which is not generally considered to be Jacobite. All glasses bearing the blackbird are prior to 1766, and it is the name by which James was familiarly known. It becomes less frequent before 1745, which suggests that Charles was already beginning to take his father's place as the centre of the Movement.

It has been suggested alternatively that the bird is a jay (for *James*), but in view of the song common in Scotland at the period of these glasses, there is less to support this theory. The song was:

> 'Oh, once on a morning of sweet recreation
> I heard a fair damsel a-making her moan,
> With sobbing and sighing and sweet lamentation,
> Aye crying, My Blackbird for ever is flown.
>
> In Scotland he's loved and dearly approved.
> In England a stranger he seemeth to be,
> But his name I'll advance in England and France,
> Good luck to my Blackbird wherever he be.'

The wild goose is another bird connected with the Jacobite cause, particularly the Irish adherents, but this has not been discovered on any glass with other Jacobite evidence.

Flowers

Where these appear in conjunction with other Jacobite emblems they almost certainly stand for those qualities normally associated with the particular flower in the age-old language of flowers. On their own they have no political significance. Numerous theories have been advanced to associate various flowers with the Jacobite movement, but these should only be accepted with considerable reservations.

The Bee

This appears regularly in glasses with the empty bud, and seems to have been adopted in the period between the two risings. As it also appears on the normal rose glasses, it has probably no essential relationship to the empty bud, but represents industry and pollination between the bud and the flower to secure a fusion. It is not in the author's view in any way related to the grub and butterfly.

The Cobweb

As in the case of the bee, this must suggest linking of the bud and flower and surely not the decay of the Movement, as has been suggested in the past. The Movement was far from dead when the cobweb first appears and it is often in conjunction with a bee or fly. Nor does one celebrate decay or willingly admit it! It was also an appropriate reminder of the lesson learnt by Robert the Bruce, which led to its becoming a royal badge of Edward III.

The Grub and Butterfly

There is an old Scots belief that the soul of a Scot will return to its native land by an underground route. The best-known expression is the ballad, supposedly sung by a Border cattle-thief due to hang in Carlisle, when his lover came to see him in prison:

> Ye'll tak the high road and I'll tak the low road
> And I'll be in Scotland afore ye,
> But I and my true love will never meet again
> On the bonny, bonny banks of Binnorie.

In order to symbolise the form in which the soul of James, or the spirit of his movement, could return underground and emerge triumphant, the Jacobites adopted the grub. This appears on a number of glasses gnawing at the flower or the stem holding it. The butterfly may represent Charles as the spirit of James returned, but a problem arises in later glasses with two butterflies and the grub. The matter is still wide open for those inclined to research, but the alternative suggestion that these glasses were mourning glasses for James is somewhat suspect in view of the real possibility that some of the glasses belong to a period before 1766. Such a date is a little late for most of them, although it is far from impossible.

The Compass

Most unusual and probably derived from the star, being in most cases later. It has been suggested that this is the badge of some club, but no evidence on the point is available.

We have now dealt with the principal emblems and may turn to some of the inscriptions appearing on the glasses. Of these by far the most common is:

Fiat (May it happen)

Originally adopted as the motto of the Cycle Club, possibly from the Old Psalter where 'Fiat' is occasionally used in place of 'Amen' at the end of a psalm, it appears that this word was later in general use as the Jacobite slogan. The extant glasses on which it is found are far too numerous and geographically widespread in origin for them to be restricted to the ambit of the Wrexham Society. In fact, their number is such that the word was probably added later in many cases, the effect of a different wheel being noticeable. How much later is debatable; the forgers have not been idle, but a glass should not be rejected as having received twentieth-century attention without a re-flection upon the possibility that the interval between the original engraving and the addition is only a few years.

Almost invariably on genuine glasses the word is written with a capital F and the remainder in minuscule letters. The F may be reversed in the Continental style. Glasses having the entire words in capital letters should be viewed with circumspection. The reason for this convention is far from clear, unless it appeared presumptuous to write what amounted to a prayer in capitals.

Redi or *Redite* and *Redeat* (Return and May he return)

As with 'Fiat', these probably originated with one specific club. From the frequency with which 'Redeat' appears in conjunction with the oak leaf it is reasonable to suspect that it originated with the Oak Society at the *Crown and Anchor* in the Strand, but again it was universally adopted, albeit with far less frequency than 'Fiat'. Such glasses number only a small percentage of those with wording.

Revirescit (He grows strong again)

Generally in conjunction with oak leaves, or an oak tree, the significance of this appears to be a reference to the House of Stuart and the prospect of a second restoration. Again such glasses are attributed to the Oak Society; they are sufficiently rare to suggest that they were peculiar to one society, but there is no extraneous evidence to support the claim of any particular society.

Success to the Society

This emblem is virtually restricted to Scottish rose glasses, the reference being to the Society of Jesus. It is late and rare.

A Health to J-ms

Perhaps the earliest form of Jacobite glass, engraved in diamond-point on glasses prior to 1725. In the very few glasses known, the inscription is accompanied by the blackbird.

3-14-5

A glass of the firing variety was encountered in France bearing this inscription, but unfortunately dismissed as a simple masonic glass. James *III* expected assistance from Louis *XIV* of France and Philip *V* of Spain and this was in all probability a Jacobite glass. No reference to such a glass can be found either in French or English bibliography, although there is a Jacobite toast to 'Job' (*James*, *Ormonde*, and *Bolingbroke*, the pillars of the '15 rebellion), and so, employing the same principle, the significance becomes clear. There was not, so far as can be ascertained, any masonic lodge using these numbers in existence during the eighteenth century.

The Glorious Memory

This normally Williamite inscription has been found on a glass *c.* 1735 engraved in diamond-point. The blackbird and bee also appear, leaving no doubt whatsoever that the Glorious Memory is not of William III.

God Bless the Prince

The only example known to the author is a plain drawn trumpet bowl with the rose and single bud. From the apparent date of the glass it is probable that this commemorates the birth of Charles.

Reddas Incolumen (May you return safely)

Again very rare, about ten known examples. Grant Francis claims that this commemorates the 1752 visit. The glasses are post 1745, but the sentiment seems ill suited to the occasion when Charles is in London, and it is preferable to regard this as a wish that a third rising may take place.

Turno tempus erit (The time will come for Turnus)

These glasses all bear the word 'Fiat' and have the rose and two buds. They date from *c.* 1750 and are probably associated with the Cycle Club, even though by this time 'Fiat' is in general use. The reference to Turnus is apt, for the woman who had been promised to Turnus was given by her father to Aeneas–a fair metaphor for the fate of the English Crown. The rest of Turnus's story is not so suitable–Turnus was killed by Aeneas!

Everso missus succurrere saeclo (Sent to succour an overthrown era)

Unusual and generally in company with a portrait and other Jacobite emblems, this has only been seen on one glass without a portrait. Eight examples have been traced. Other inscriptions occur in conjunction with portraits and are accordingly treated in the following section.

PORTRAIT GLASSES

These, the fifth class of Jacobite glasses, became popular about 1750, and it will therefore be no surprise to learn that James does not appear in more than two extant glasses. Charles, however, is a frequent subject – both in England and abroad – for wheel-engraving, the portrait normally being framed by a laurel-wreath. In many glasses he is shown wearing the Garter ribbon over the wrong shoulder, and it is possible that some of these glasses were engraved abroad; certainly one or two are foreign glasses. An interesting view was put forward by Bles that the direction in which Charles faces is governed by the numismatic convention that rulers face the opposite direction to their predecessor. Grant Francis, whose knowledge of coins was considerable, disagreed, and although the majority do face one way (over the right shoulder), there are a few full face – of which one also bears the unique inscription 'Carolus' – and several in which the Prince looks to his left. Inscriptions are limited. 'Hic Vir, Hic Est' (This, this is the man) is the rarest, and 'Audentior Ibo' (I will go more boldly) the commonest. Even so the reader must not imagine that such glasses are by any means frequent. Portraits of Flora Macdonald occur but are exceedingly rare.

Finally mention must be made of the six known colour-enamelled portraits of Charles, which (apart from unique specimens and perhaps the 'Hic Vir, Hic Est' portrait glasses) must be the rarest class of Jacobite glasses. They date between 1755 and 1775 and must be regarded as truly exceptional.

Jacobite glass is essentially a matter for research and speculation. There is still much to be discovered and the authorities differ considerably. The reader is therefore well advised to keep an open mind, but to remember also that this class of drinking glass is the forger's paradise.

A second and less extensive class of commemorative glasses is the Williamite series. There has been singularly little research into this subject, and the only recognised forms are the portrait and the inscribed glasses.

When William of Orange landed at Torbay he was welcomed not for his own personality, which by all accounts was unsympathetic, but because he represented Protestantism. His conquests in Ireland and particularly the Battle of the Boyne in 1690 were celebrated by the Protestant minority in Ireland for the next seventy or eighty years. In Ulster his praises could be sung without fear, but in the rest of the country the meetings of Orange supporters were necessarily as secret as the Jacobite meetings in England. It is probable that most of the early Williamite glasses were made for masonic lodges in Ireland and that the emblems gained currency in England at a somewhat later date. The toast which appears on many glasses was 'THE EVER GLORIOUS AND IMMORTAL MEMORY OF KING WILLIAM III.', and the majority of the known glasses are busts or equestrian portraits, the latter much outnumbering the former. The toast appeared in many abbreviated forms, and reference to the Boyne was relatively frequent.

Just what the secret emblems were, if indeed there were any, has not been discovered, but a surprising number of masonic firing glasses show a bird which an ornithologist has identified as a 'deformed snipe'. Now, the snipe is a bird which in writings of the time was, and still is, commonly associated with the marsh-lands of Holland, and there is one eighteenth-century reference to a group of Protestant gentlemen after a shoot in Ireland drinking to the snipe. Why this bird in particular? It may be fanciful to read political significance into this action, but if this is justified it may help to explain some of the birds on Jacobite glasses which fly along as if their necks are broken—a very apt reference to the desired fate of William's successors. For those inclined to research this may well prove a fruitful field.

The period of Williamite glasses is very much longer, and starts earlier, than the Jacobite, but the market would be virtu-ally restricted to Ireland and a few were certainly made there. Grant Francis goes further and says, 'practically all Orange glasses have an Irish origin', but this is not a contention for which there is much evidence and it probably pleased some Englishmen to show their loyalty to the House of Orange at a time when Jacobitism was rife. There was no need to disguise the glasses at all, and many of the more extravagant glasses were undoubtedly made in England.

Commemorative glass is generally of more value than that bearing other forms of engraved decoration and the field for the collector (and forger) is wide. A number of glasses exist in which the style and the event commemorated are wholly incompatible. Not all these are to be condemned, for some events are recognised only later as memorable, but the collector must know his history as well as his glass if he is to avoid expensive error. This type of glass cannot easily be divided into categories nor can limits of nationality always be set, for we know that some Jacobite glasses were engraved abroad and that Newcastle glasses were often exported to Holland and engraved there. Foreign sentiments on English glass are not unknown, nor English sentiments on foreign glass. We are here concerned, however, with the range of English glasses of the eighteenth century or earlier which bear engraved commemoration of English events, things, or periods. All are rare, some being unique, and the reader must not assume from what follows that such pieces are to be found easily.

Royalty naturally has attracted the engraver and every sovereign from Charles II onwards is noted. Glasses commemorative of coronations far exceed others, save in the case of William III, and death glasses are most uncommon. Princes and queens receive far less attention. The royal coat of arms is found on surprisingly few examples prior to the nineteenth century.

Some extremely well-executed engravings for private families are to be found—crests, ciphers, and coats of arms being the most common form—although marriage glasses appear to have had periods of favour, the majority being executed in diamond-point. Similarly towns and cities are often represented by their arms.

Trade and masonic glasses abound, those of the city guilds being among the most sought after. Here the standard of engraving is frequently very high. Other non-political communities such as hunts or drinking clubs often had their own engraved glass. Religious sentiments are infrequently noted.

Regimental glasses or others with military significance are far more numerous in Ireland than elsewhere, but are completely outnumbered by naval examples. Ships, events, and men are all represented, and a fairly large body of 'privateer' glasses exists, fourteen ships not in the Navy lists being noted.

Those of which more than one specimen has been encountered are the *Eagle*, the *Providence*, the *Mary*, the *Renown* (although this name appears also in the Navy lists), the *Joyous*, the *Adventure*, and the *Lion*. Admirals, particularly Byng, are noted, although examples are rare. Battles are even rarer and three modern engravings of 'Gibraltar' glasses suggest that this class merits more than usual circumspection.

Political causes have attracted perhaps the most attention, the cause of John Wilkes giving rise to a number of 'Wilkes and Liberty' glasses. Election glasses wishing success to various candidates are for the most part late in the century, but some early examples have been noted. A recently encountered glass of this type dated 1722 is remarkable for the extent by which it predates all other known examples. American independence and certain treaties are duly commemorated.

Trade and sport are widely marked, the former appearing more frequently as the Industrial Revolution gathered strength and particularly later in the eighteenth century. A wide variety of sports is represented, hunting and racing predominating. Occasionally a particularly fine horse or hound is the subject of an engraved glass, the earliest dated example of this type encountered being 1793.

Innumerable other subjects exist, but to draw up a definitive list is impossible. The collector will quite possibly never come across some of the classes mentioned above, but find more than one example of a class here ignored. The frequency of commemorative glass as a percentage of all eighteenth-century glass is fractional, and quite apart from the aesthetic appeal and possible rarity of such pieces they provide in many cases a most attractive field for research. Who, for example, is Henry Heston that he should be commemorated on an opaque-twist glass with his name over crossed swords? Who was S.I., who married Mr Hutchinson of Stony Gill in 1764? The interest of such glasses is not limited to glass collectors.

For further reference:

STEEVENSON, M. Papers read to *The Circle of Glass Collectors* on *Jacobite Glass* (the most authoritative research on the Jacobite Period).
And see Bibliography.

CHAPTER TEN

Notes on English Glass of the Eighteenth Century

THE collection of notes which follows is designed primarily to assist in the recognition of eighteenth-century English glass, and to expose the more obvious failings of modern imitations. Some of the more common Continental characteristics are noted, and the graph and diagrams will assist in classifying drinking glasses.

The notes cannot be comprehensive, and the experienced collector will recognise the exceptions that occur to every general rule set down here. This chapter is therefore addressed principally to the beginner, in order that the most common mistakes may be avoided until such time as instinct can supplement basic knowledge. Such instinct can only develop through the continual handling and close observation of old glass, and it is always fallible.

There are four main features which must be taken into account when inspecting a piece of glass and they are, in order of importance:

1. The Metal.
2. The Proportions.
3. The Wear.
4. The Decoration.

Of these four features the most difficult for the beginner to recognise is the first, and until the colour of the metal can be recognised as a matter of course it is inadvisable to purchase expensive pieces.

The proportions can be learnt from books, and it is with this in mind that the line-drawings have been included. The classification is in accordance with the excellent scheme of definition drawn up by Barrington Haynes in *Glass through the Ages*, and the drawings so far as possible refer to the average shape, although, of course, there is no absolute standard.

The problems of wear-marks and decoration are explained in sections which to a certain extent reiterate matter appearing earlier in this volume; while the graph, chronology (see page 190), and notes on cleaning and repairing are included for the convenience of the reader.

THE METAL

Soda-metal is generally lighter in weight than lead-metal, and a glass in soda-metal will look heavier than it feels. Experience is of course the best guide, but on occasion even the expert will hesitate. In order to be certain, there is a chemical test which the collector can employ without serious detriment, provided extreme care is used; the test should not, however, be tried unless every other means has failed. Dip a clean cocktail stick in hydrofluoric acid and touch the base of the glass, the ideal place being on the pontil mark. Taking another stick, dip it in sulphide of ammonia and touch the same spot. A white reaction indicates soda-metal, a black or brown reaction lead. Immediately remove the chemicals either by drying or preferably with plenty of water. Since this test can create hazing on the metal, only minute quantities of chemical should be used in an unobtrusive spot, and the glass should never be left with them on. Since hydrofluoric acid is dangerously corrosive, the test is not recommended as a normal course.

Horizontal striation is to be seen in the bowl in some degree in every early glass, but it will not normally be as emphatic as that in the foot. At the rim of the bowl it is not uncommon to find slight vertical striation. Tooling-marks may also exist where the top of the bowl has been opened out. Examination under ultra-violet light is ideal for the inspection of striation.

The colour of English lead-metal follows a fairly definite pattern, but it is essential that the glass should be viewed by daylight, preferably against a white background. Artificial light can be wickedly misleading. The tints generally to be expected are green up to 1690, black, steel-blue, and grey up to 1740. A yellow, pink, or brown cast is more consistent with Continental glass and a white cast is alien to the eighteenth century. A hard clear tint is modern.

The feel of the metal is a form of guidance which can only be the result of experience, but an old metal will generally feel 'softer', if one can thus describe the sensation, while lacking the smooth, greasy feel of modern glass. Weight, colour, and feel are all tests which necessitate the handling of old glass at every opportunity over a long period before they become reliable guides.

Crizzling is not necessarily a sign of old glass, for the fault is still prevalent in the nineteenth century, particularly abroad. In English glass it is only to be expected in early light metal, and the collector is advised not to rely on its presence as indicative of anything except faulty batch.

Making the metal ring by flicking it with a finger-nail is perhaps the most fallacious test of glass yet devised. The absence of a 'ring' does not necessarily indicate that the glass is not lead; a lead glass may not ring if the build-up of the metal is inferior. The only guidance which a ring can give is the absence of serious damage to the bowl and the fact that the glass is reasonably well made.

Finally the collector is warned against the so-called 'distinctive' blue of Waterford glass. This distinction is a myth, for within ten years of Waterford producing metal with a bluish tint, in any event by no means exclusive to Waterford, it was being accurately reproduced abroad, particularly at Lyons. There are more examples of so-called 'eighteenth-century Waterford' glass on the market today than could ever have been made in Waterford during the limited period of glassmaking there in the eighteenth century. Guidance in this field must come from the shapes and cutting.

THE BOWL

We have already seen that striation is to be expected in the bowl and wear-marks may exist on the rim if the glass has been stored upside-down; a bowl without minor scratch-marks on its walls is unusual. Occasionally the rim is ground to eliminate a chip, but such grinding will be obvious to the touch and sight, for the slight thickening of the metal at the rim, caused in manufacture when the glass is held to the furnace to eliminate the sharp sheared edge, will be absent.

With the exception of those bowls where the base is solid, or the bottom of the bowl is of a diameter which permits the convenient use of tools inside, one may expect in early glasses to find a slightly convex hump inside the bowl above the stem.

Where it does exist, the crevices are unlikely to be without some slight patina.

The bell and waisted bowl were extremely popular in Holland, but seldom included a solid base; the type endured much longer on the Continent than in England. Opaque-twists with a bell bowl are a common Dutch form, the bell opening out fairly sharply at the rim in contrast to the more gradual opening of the English style. Although the bell is relatively common in England, even in opaque-twists, it is almost always early and more delicately proportioned.

One feature of bowls which has hitherto received little attention is the opaque bloom which hazes the metal. There are four principal reasons for this, of which three are fairly obvious. Crizzling, which has been mentioned earlier, is easily identifiable, since its appearance will be over-all and in its advanced stages gives the glass a crazed look. In the early stages it is a thin film and temporarily removable. Also identifiable is the ghost of gilt fixative, which, even if the gilt is gone, retains the definite pattern. Gilding was not popular in England in the eighteenth century, and instances of this sort of hazing are not particularly frequent.

Haze created by wear may take two forms, abrasion of the surface from use and cleaning, and attack on the metal by the contents of the vessel. The former can often be removed by the use of jeweller's rouge, but in general is best left. The latter may respond to a mild detergent after a period of soaking in distilled water, but abrasive detergents are to be avoided at all costs.

One of the commonest causes of hazing is, however, the reheating of the glass at the 'glory-hole' during the shaping. The higher the lead content of the glass the less likely becomes this phenomenon. The highest incidence falls in the period of glass with a low lead content or in soda-metal after the introduction of coal as a fuel, i.e. the seventeenth century. The hazing is caused by sulphur attack from the flame, and in general will be found below the rim of the bowl, where the rim has been reheated on shearing and the sulphur at the outside of the flame has not been consumed. A similar hazing may occasionally be found on the foot.

There is no cure for sulphur hazing and it is indicative of poor manufacturing technique, for it will not occur where the furnace used for finishing is kept at a sufficiently high temperature to eliminate the sulphur in the furnace atmosphere. There is no test for this feature that excludes all other causes, but it will occasionally explain an otherwise unidentifiable hazing. Obviously one expects to find it close to those parts of the glass where there has been shaping or shearing rather than on a plain section.

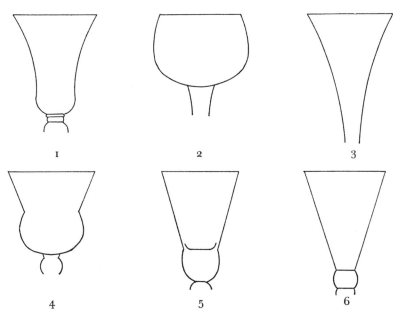

FIG. 9 English eighteenth-century bowl shapes

The bowl forms as illustrated:

1. *The Bell.* Generally early in England, it endured for a much longer period on the Continent and in America. The *waisted* bowl is essentially similar and the term includes those bowls which are either elongated or abbreviated. The solid-based versions of both bell and waisted bowls are in general earlier than those without the solid base. The style dies out in England by about 1760.
2. *The Cup.* One of the rarer forms dating to the first half of the eighteenth century, with occasional specimens later. Commonest on plain-stemmed and incised-twist glasses.

3. *The Trumpet.* Apparent throughout the eighteenth century, the deeper bowl being on the whole earlier. Common to all groups.
4. *The Thistle.* In its hollow form generally late. More common in the smaller glasses, but never very popular.
5. *The Solid-based Thistle.* Again very early, tending to lapse after about 1740.
6. *The V or Conical.* One of the earliest shapes (often with a solid base in early glass), which continued throughout the period.

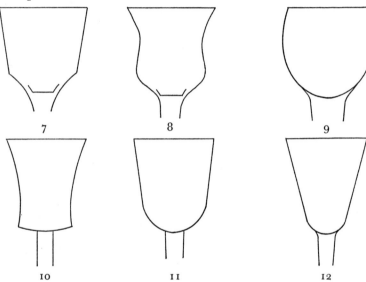

FIG. 10 English eighteenth-century bowl shapes

7. *The Ogee.* Certainly the most popular shape of the twist groups. More common in the middle of the century than at the beginning or end.
8. *The Waisted Ogee.* Much less common and on the whole slightly later than the straightforward ogee.
9. *The Ovoid.* A late shape and extremely common from 1750 onwards.
10. *The Bucket.* Popular, but not as frequent as either the ogee or the ovoid. Appears also in a waisted form. Predominantly late and not frequent in groups other than the air- and opaque-twists.

11. *The Round Funnel.* Popular throughout the century after about 1720. All groups.
12. *The Pointed Round Funnel.* A variation of the above, commencing slightly later.

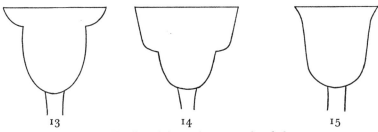

13   14   15

FIG. 11 English eighteenth-century bowl shapes

13. *The Saucer-topped Round Funnel.* A complex bowl appearing in the period of twist stems. Not frequent, and rare in other groups.
14. *The Pan-topped Round Funnel.* An extension of the above, with some glasses coming between the two categories. Commoner than 13 above.
15. *The Lipped Round Funnel.* As above, but far less frequent.

THE FOOT

In English glass, with the exception of champagne-glasses, the foot is almost invariably of equal or greater diameter than the bowl. The early folded foot is wider then the late, and over-all the tendency is to a wider fold than was favoured on the Continent. Where the foot is conical the glass will stand only on the extreme outer edge of the foot, as is normally evidenced by the wear-marks. This characteristic is a distinctive feature of English eighteenth-century glass, for Continental and American feet tend to be flatter. On a plain foot one may expect to encounter the same phenomenon, and a further test for a good glass is to rub one's finger over the edge from the top, where no angled edge is discernible. Rubbing one's finger up from below will reveal the sharper angle of the edge. The absence of this angular edge, or the presence of one on the upper surface, should put one on one's guard against a later glass or a glass of which the foot has been ground to remove a chip. The domed foot may have the same feature, although here the glass does not necessarily rest on its extreme outer edge. Under magnification, wear-marks (which must be present unless the glass is virtually unused) will appear as a series of scratches running in every direction. Wear-marks imposed on a later glass will show a tendency to run in groups in one direction, where the glass has been drawn over an abrasive surface to simulate genuine marks. The severity of wear-marks will, of course, vary in accordance with the weight of the glass.

The pontil mark, where the pontil has been broken off under the end of the stem, is to be expected on all glass prior to the faceted-stem period and many faceted examples still have unground pontil marks. The custom of grinding and polishing off the rough fracture was adopted a little earlier on the Continent, and is common on French opaque-twists. As feet in time became flatter, quite clearly this protruding stub had to be removed, but all early eighteenth-century blown glass should still have the mark. Discoloration round the pontil mark is common in early glass, and trapped dirt is to be expected in crevices caused by the fracture. The same may be expected in the joint of the folded foot. Visible striation running round the foot is common in the eighteenth century until *c.* 1780, and a foot without any irregularity or visible striation of the metal invites closer inspection of its other features.

Some research into dating by the angle of the conical foot has

a) Plain, Conical   b) Folded

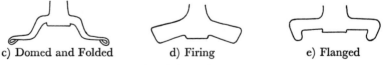

c) Domed and Folded   d) Firing   e) Flanged

FIG. 12 English eighteenth-century foot shapes

revealed no regular development within the century, but the absence of any conical form, or a particularly flat base section to the domed foot, should be treated as late, unless other features contradict.

The foot forms shown in Fig. 12 are those most common during the eighteenth century. The domed foot appears also without the fold, but seems to occur predominantly in glasses made of a fragile metal that chips. To some extent this failing may also be attributable to the inherently weaker structure of the domed foot. The domed and folded is probably later than the plain domed, and appeared as a solution to this problem.

THE STEM

In the baluster groups one may expect to find tooling marks or minor imperfections of finish. Knopping which upsets the proportions of the whole is unusual in the eighteenth century, and a long straight section with simple knopping or collaring beneath the bowl is a late development which continued into the early nineteenth century. While on the subject of proportion, one must also expect in glasses of certain shapes a deviation from plumb in the stem during annealing. Modern annealing methods reduce or eliminate this failing, so that the collector may take this into consideration in conjunction with other factors.

The knops shown in Fig. 13 are those most likely to be encountered. They are shown with tears in knop forms where a tear is usual.

(*a*) The Simple Knop.
(*b*) The True Baluster.
(*c*) The Inverted Baluster.
(*d*) The Egg Knop.
(*e*) The Cylinder Knop.
(*f*) The Cone Knop.
(*g*) The Acorn Knop.
(*h*) The Mushroom Knop.
(*i*) The Annulated Knop.
(*j*) The Dumb-bell.
(*k*) The Angular Knop.

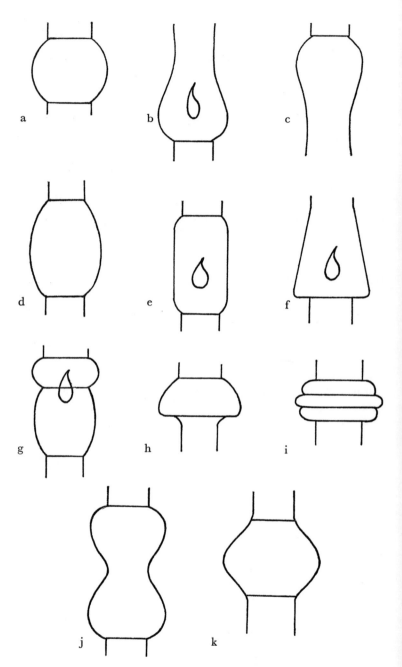

FIG. 13 English Baluster period knop shapes

Both air- and opaque-twist stems invariably have the twist rising from the left up to the right and were made as part of and at the same time as the rest of the stem. Continental twists do not adhere to this apparently inflexible rule of the English twist. Reproductions often reveal their two-part manufacture by the trapping of air pockets in the recesses of a cable twist. The true eighteenth-century twist is always encased in clear metal before twisting, and the diameter of the stem is not enlarged by recasing.

The English had no real rivals in the opaque-twist field in the eighteenth century, and even now few reproductions achieve comparable standards. The Dutch and Norwegian twists are generally of a less pure white, rather like well-watered milk; and the French copies, being later, reveal their source by their flat foot structure, the pontil mark often being polished smooth. Coloured twists have always been a rarity and the only English colours known to the author are blue (most common), red, brown, green, and yellow (rarest). Variations in the depth of colour are many, but combinations generally include white– except for a blue, red, and green twist which is late in the period. Combination colour-twists of inferior quality are frequently found to be foreign, for in this country the colour-twists are the final development of a mastered art.

The spirals of an English opaque-twist should be close to the circumference of the stem and the surrounding clear glass should scarcely add to the diameter, unless of course the twist is simply a central cable or other particularly compact design. The same applies to the air-twist.

The hollow-stem and incised-twist periods present little difficulty in recognition and no intentional forgeries have been noted. Neither style has a true Continental counterpart.

The faceted-stem period is remarkably free from the problems presented by the forgers. It represents too much work for a finished product which is unlikely to obtain a record price. The glasses of this category have a number of features which assist not only in dating but also in assessing the craftsmanship. Stems are normally short and straight. A single knop may appear in the middle or at the top, and the cutting continues over this. The facets are normally diamonds longer than they are broad, thus necessitating less facets than equal quadrilaterals would to cover the stem. The hexagon cut served the same purpose. Faceting continues on to the bowl, ending in rounded flutes which tend, in glasses dating late in the eighteenth century, to be fairly shallow. Shell or scale facet-cutting seems to have become popular in this country only late in the period. Most examples of glasses intended to deceive the collector have facets with acute angles, which deprives them of the flowing line found in the genuine eighteenth-century article. The collector should also check facet-stem glasses for damage, since many examples sold as perfect have damage to the stem which is not immediately apparent, the most frequent point of failure being the facet angles which stand slightly proud.

The tendency of copyists and reproducers, whether their intention is to deceive or not, is to improve and perhaps produce a rarity. The result is normally either an ill-proportioned glass, which would have offended eighteenth-century taste, or such a freak style that the collector will in any event be put upon his guard; for the styles follow a definite pattern and reproduction will often evolve a glass with features chronologically incompatible.

THE STEM PERIODS

The definitions adopted here are those of Barrington Haynes, whose book *Glass through the Ages* is the most accurate classification of eighteenth-century drinking glasses. The limits set by Haynes are marked, in each case, above those set by the author, and it will be seen that the tendency of the present author is to set slightly earlier dates. It must be remembered that in each case the dates reflect the main period of currency, and earlier and later examples may be expected. The notes following explain why the different dates are given.

MOULDED PEDESTAL

Haynes extends the period to 1765, which coincided with the close of the Newcastle style. The rather leggy moulded stems attributed to Newcastle tend to display the techniques employed up to the middle of the century and almost certainly died out before the true Newcastle style, which fulfilled an export demand besides catering for English taste. By 1750 new forms were

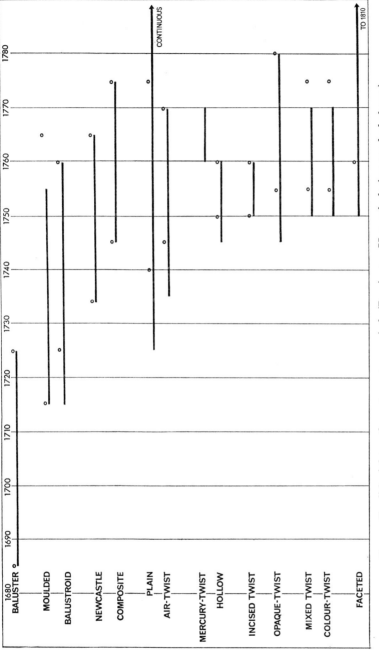

FIG. 14 English eighteenth-century stem periods (Barrington Haynes's dating marked above.)

ousting the knopped stems, and the moulded pedestal had no place among the more refined varieties.

BALUSTROID

The distinction here is less real than would appear and results from the division by Haynes of baluster and balustroid, a division which is unreal in that the same style gradually became lighter. It is, perhaps, more realistic to allow the periods some considerable overlap.

PLAIN

Here it is dubious whether any limits at all should be set, and the date 1725 has been chosen as that of the earliest dated example known. Probably some plain stems were made even prior to 1700, but, since the same style endures for most of the eighteenth century, dating is exceptionally difficult.

AIR-TWIST

During the course of research, a letter from Francis Buckley to the Oldham Museum strengthened the opinion that an earlier date should be set to this group. What influenced Buckley to say 1737 is not clear, but possibly he believed that the air-twist was the height of fashion during the period of maximum Jacobite activity between about 1737 and 1745. Certainly many of the disguised Jacobite air-twist glasses are more explicable if one is permitted to date them prior to 1745.

HOLLOW

Here the difference is minimal and perhaps unnecessary, but the style may have originated from the Excise Acts of 1745–6.

OPAQUE-TWIST

Again the question of Jacobite emblems makes an earlier date desirable, since many of the opaque-twist Jacobite glasses bear the signs of the really active period around 1745 and not the fading cause of 1755–60, by which time the emblems are becoming more specialised.

MIXED AND COLOUR-TWISTS

As a result of dating other groups slightly earlier than Haynes, these may be brought into line. The distinction here is mechanical rather than essential.

FACETED STEMS

Just how early faceting began is not clear, but there is evidence to suggest that it was brought from Bohemia in 1727. The advance of dates is therefore probably inadequate; but the earliest engraved and dated example known is 1751, by which date the style may possibly have already been well established.

The principal object of the graph is to show at a glance the styles which one may expect to encounter at any given period. It will be observed, perhaps with some surprise, that between 1750 and 1760 all the formations are to be seen, with the exception of the baluster and the mercury-twist, and even this latter form was probably emerging. The extent to which the Excise Acts influenced this transitional period is unfortunately impossible to assess.

THE FREQUENCY OF EIGHTEENTH-CENTURY WINEGLASSES

The table drawn up below is based on an analysis of catalogue lists from three major sale-rooms over a period of four years. It may be that a fallacious result has been obtained, but prices tend to confirm the general impression gained from a numerical survey, allowing a certain margin for aesthetic value.

Certain difficulties arise which alter the picture. For example, rudimentary stems appear to be commonest, but they are also the most difficult to attribute with certainty to the eighteenth century. To a lesser extent the position of the faceted stem may be similarly affected. Balusters and balustroids merge and together are as numerous as, or slightly more frequent than, air-twists. Only the very heavy balusters have been classed as such, and any borderline cases remitted to the balustroid group. Similarly attribution to the Newcastle group has been sparing, thus increasing the balustroid group.

The resulting order of frequency, commencing with the most common is:

1. Rudimentary.
2. Plain.
3. Opaque-twist.
4. Air-twist.
5. Balustroid.
6. Faceted.
7. Baluster.
8. Newcastle baluster.
9. Moulded pedestal.
10. Composite (Air).
11. Mixed twist.
12. Incised twist.
13. Composite (Opaque).
14. Colour-twist.
15. Hollow.

Within the groups, other than those where knopping is a group feature, knopped specimens are always less frequent than plain stems. Foot frequency runs thus: plain, folded, domed, domed and folded, firing, and last the specialist forms, although this frequency does not apply to drams and other small glasses, and the whole picture is governed by dating. Bowl frequency is impossible to analyse, although the simple forms are in all groups more common than the complex, such as the saucer-top and pan-topped round funnel. Moulded bowls (except in the moulded pedestal group) are not common, and a moulded complex bowl is, in general, rare.

ENGRAVING

This should always be judged against a white background, preferably set directly on the reverse side of the engraved part. The finish of wheel-engraving should not have the smoothness attainable with a modern power-driven wheel, and should have at least a mild patina and possibly wear-marks at the edges. A metallic sheen may be evidence that the engraved part was once gilded – this will have the effect of making the engraving grey rather than muddy brown. A clear almost white effect is essentially modern.

Some of the above features can only be examined under a strong magnifying-glass, which will often reveal a modern attempt to age the engraving by rubbing with dust or jeweller's rouge. The desirability of using a magnifying-glass on engraved glasses cannot be stressed enough.

The subject-matter of the engraving will also give some guidance. Some years ago a magnificent 'Jacobite' glass was encountered. The glass was undoubtedly mid-eighteenth century, but the engraving modern. The forger, for in this case intent to deceive was obvious, had not been content to embrace a limited number of emblems, and the result was a feast of emblems of all periods, and one or two new ones. Had he exercised reasonable restraint, the engraver might conceivably have averted the extremely close scrutiny that his exuberance ensured.

Modern glasses with modern engraving will be apparent on even casual inspection, unless the metal is an accurate reproduction; this is rarely the case, for it would then show no profit. Foreign engraving on a glass of English shape and metal makes it no less desirable, provided that the engraving is contemporaneous with the glass. It should be borne in mind that wheel-engraving only became accepted in this country after 1720.

Acid etching, which was not an eighteenth-century technique, is occasionally used by the forger to improve the effect of his wheel-engraving. This will be evident where the outline lacks the defined edge which would be left by the wheel.

Diamond-point stippling is a process unlikely to appeal to the forger, but ordinary diamond-point engraving, as in the 'Amen' glasses, is relatively simple to reproduce and the collector should not be tempted into this sort of purchase without considerable experience. Dating of diamond-point engraving is virtually impossible, but one may try the same tests as on wheel-engraving to decide whether the engraving is old or very new.

ENAMELLING

The colouring of the enamel is of paramount importance. Wear is to be expected and any pitting should contain some fouling.

This is a field which does not appeal to the forger of eighteenth-century glass, since there is no easy way to simulate age. A few 'Beilby Armorials' exist, but these are generally on inferior twist stems and in one case include a nineteenth-century coat of arms. Foreign enamelling is generally of weaker colouring, or else has a Germanic brashness totally unlike the English styles.

GILDING

It is far from clear how popular this was in England in the eighteenth century. Certainly there are glasses with the shadow left where gilding has worn off, but the decoration only becomes common in the faceted-stem period. Although gilding was evidently used on engraving, few examples retaining the gilt exist, and it is probable that the art of permanent gilding was not generally known in Great Britain until about 1800 – although surface gilding was certainly known prior to the time of Verzelini. On the Continent gilding was common from an early date, but was not normally used on glasses which can be confused with the English styles.

CUTTING AND MOULDING

Cutting has far greater limitations than moulding, and this will be apparent if one considers the technique of cutting. The glass is held to the wheel, so that there will be certain areas of the glass which cannot be reached by the wheel (e.g. on a jug close to the handle), whereas the making of the mould imposes no such limitation. Secondly, the circular cutter cannot bring a groove to an abrupt end – a groove must become shallow at its extremities where the wheel is lifted out. Thirdly, accuracy is not normally wholly attained in cutting, particularly where grooves radiate from a central point. There can be no correction of error and some irregularity is inevitable, whereas the mould-maker can perfect his mould before it is used at all. Press-moulded glass will generally show a seam or (if this has been concealed) some feature of the pattern which allows for the seam. Sharpness of design and angle tends to be lost in the moulding process, and circular designs, virtually impossible of execution with a cutting-wheel, are found in abundance.

The distinctive form of cutting so often attributed to Ireland is predominantly nineteenth century, and the characteristics have been fully treated in other books. In the period with which this section of the book is concerned, the author does not accept the arguments that Irish glass developed on exclusive lines.

CLEANING GLASS

We have already seen that scratch-marks can be eliminated to some extent with jeweller's rouge, although the practice is in general to be avoided. There are many cases where glass has stain-marks or dirt which can be lifted without detriment to the metal.

The first, and most desirable, means of removing marks is the use of distilled water, in which the piece should be left to soak. Gentle rubbing with a cloth or very soft brush will then often remove marks which remained fast after normal washing. The use of liquid detergents, such as are used for dish-washing, will not harm the glass, but the use of detergents bought in powder or paste form is not desirable, since many contain a mildly abrasive element. Enamelled glasses should not be subjected to detergent treatment.

No attempt should be made to scrape a mark off the glass—it may have adhered during manufacture, and damage, or at least an ugly refractive mark, can result. If the mark cannot be removed easily with a thumb-nail after washing or soaking, it is best to leave it.

Decanters or other pieces, where it is difficult to get at the area to be cleaned, can sometimes be treated with a solution of a denture cleaner, although a prior test on other glass is recommended. Some cleaners have been found harmful. The normally accepted abrasive methods (e.g. with sand and water, or lead shot and water) are not desirable and should be used only as a last resort.

After thorough rinsing in water, those parts which cannot be dried with a cloth should be rinsed with methylated spirit, which will evaporate without streaks. The temperature of water used to clean old glass should not be more than tepid. Modern glass, being on the whole better annealed, is less sensitive. If hot water is used, the temperature should be built up gradually from tepid

with the glass in the water throughout. Before washing enamelled glass one must be certain that it is fire-enamelling; much
nineteenth-century opaque glass is only surface-painted in
materials soluble in water.

Glass which has been buried should not be washed until
expert advice has been sought; surface decoration may well
adhere to the surrounding soil as much as to the glass.

REPAIRING GLASS

Any repair undertaken by the collector himself should not be such
that it prevents improvement by others at a later date. The use
of rivets is abominable, and some of the modern adhesives are
not only equally effective but also far less disfiguring. Where
repairs are to be done professionally, the collector is advised to
ensure, before having the work done, that he fully appreciates
the nature of the repair. All too often he will find that the restored article is not as he envisaged, owing to the introduction of
new metal or more extensive removal of the old. This is in no
way a criticism of those firms that restore glass, but rather of the
collector who fails to ascertain exactly what will be done.
Advice should also be sought on the desirability of repair – the
piece in its damaged state may still be more valuable and
interesting than if it were repaired.

CHAPTER ELEVEN

Glass after 1800

THE recognised date at which the period of 'antiques' ends is still 1830. This date is arbitrary and so far as glass is concerned wholly unrelated to any phasing in the history of its development, for the very beginning of the nineteenth century is marked by an international boom in the industry and a surge of interest in the glass art forms. In almost every country glass now becomes an accepted medium, not only for luxury goods but also for the utility ware of even the least prosperous household. Industrial advance and improved communications bring a formerly expensive commodity within the reach of all and provide the means of mass production.

For the collector this presents a number of hazards. Not only does it become increasingly difficult to create a collection which is truly representative without it becoming too large, but also it becomes more difficult to date pieces with any degree of accuracy unless they fall within a few defined categories. Much has been written on various aspects of the development of glass in the nineteenth century, and in the compass of this chapter it is impossible to do more than mention a few of the more prominent achievements; the reader who considers collecting glass of this period must look for detailed guidance elsewhere.

The English quality glass of this age is superb metal – solid, cut to show off its refractive powers, and expensive-looking. That any single artist should emerge and endure is remarkable, but one figure appears whose achievements cannot be ignored. Apsley Pellatt (1791–1863) was the greatest exponent of a form which commands attention for its technical merit, if not for its artistic quality, called *crystallo-ceramie*.

The basic principle of *crystallo-ceramie* is the enclosure of a decorative ceramic bas-relief in a lustrous block of clear glass, which may then be treated in a variety of ways.

Pellatt took out a patent for this process in 1819, when he had overcome the problem which had dogged the earlier Bohemian exponents of the art. The ceramic bas-relief and the glass tended to contract unequally during annealing, with the result that distortion was frequent, but Pellatt overcame this by adjusting the components of the ceramic part. Since a great deal of Pellatt's work was portraiture of royalty, any distortion was disastrous.

Such was the popular hunger for art glass that we find *crystallo-ceramie* used in paper-weights, doorknobs, ear-rings, and bottle stoppers, to name only a few of its forms. Nor will the reader be surprised that the glass block was submitted to the sometimes none too tender mercies of the cutter. Perhaps things went too far, for the art suffered a decline in about 1830; it was however far from dead.

In 1845 the Glass Excise Acts were repealed and for a short time thereafter *crystallo-ceramie* enjoyed favour again and, although many glasshouses made examples, few achieved the standards set by Pellatt before reaction set in against the heaviness of the style.

The latter part of the nineteenth century is marked by a return to lighter metals and shallower cutting (see Plate 118), decoration now being considered an integral and virtually indispensable part of glassmaking. The causes of this reaction are many, but one of the principal reasons was probably the development of press-moulded glass. This American process meant that the hitherto expensive cut glass could be copied cheaply by the use of a mould ridged to impress like cutting. Generally the moulded copy is unlikely to be mistaken for cut glass, for reasons which are set out elsewhere, but a few fine examples do exist which must have been almost as expensive to make as cut glass, for they are finished with a cutting-wheel.

A further aspect of the reaction was that William Morris and others like him were seeking to return to the individual accomplishments of the craftsmen. In the field of glass, Morris employed the Whitefriars Glass Company to make him a set of table-glass to the design of Philip Webb, who was also the architect of the 'Red House'. The example thus set had less influence than some might wish, and although Whitefriars sought to propagate the gospel in the years that followed, few firms broke entirely with the past demand. The drinking glass of the nineteenth century is by modern standards still impressive and opulent-looking, but the artistic merit is infinitely variable.

In the range of ornamental glass there were considerable

successes in a number of fields, notably coloured glass. Here the treatment of the medium was infinitely more artistic, and the desire to impress far more subtle. There is a tendency to connect early coloured glass exclusively with Bristol, but it must be remembered that this is a century of industrial growth and improving communications, in which a local style could not for long remain local if it had any merit. Thus when one speaks of Bristol glass one is speaking of a fashion and not necessarily of provenance.

Bristol, where glass had been made over a long period – there were nine glasshouses there in 1696 – was a centre which had gained a very considerable reputation in the eighteenth century for its excellent clear flint, and we know that coloured glass was made there as early as 1750; the nineteenth century, however, sees the peak of Bristol's achievement. This is no indictment of the eighteenth-century coloured products but rather a change in popular taste. The Jacobs family, in the latter part of the eighteenth century, had been producing blue glass which was of a very high standard; and at one time Michael Edkins, the enameller, worked for them as a gilder. Opaque-white glass dates back to the same period and has a different texture from the Continental opaline. It is both softer to look at and the white is creamier than the foreign product. Enamelling was perhaps the *raison d'être* of Bristol opaque-white, and a great deal of dressing-table ware and table-bottles can be found which date back prior to 1800. Candlesticks were among the earlier items to be made, but since the fashions of opaque-white endured, it is difficult to ascribe an accurate date to any given piece. Contemporary designs on pottery often give us the best guidance, and the Regency inclination to the oriental can be found repeated on glass. The opaque-white also lent itself admirably to surface painting, and a great many charming designs were painted on, only to be lost or partially obliterated over the years by cleaning. The collector should remember that, on the whole, Bristol glass has a very high lead content–much of the opaque-white is potash-lead metal–and could be blown very thinly without detriment to appearance, while many of the centres that imitated Bristol just did not achieve the technical standards of the metal.

The name of Nailsea has now become synonymous with a

style; and it is right that this should be so, for here again the original products were grossly outnumbered by the imitations which immediately flowed from other centres. It is exceptionally difficult to identify true Nailsea, which was made at a village of that name some eight or nine miles out of Bristol, from copies made in Bristol, Stourbridge, and elsewhere. This is no reflection on Bristol or Stourbridge, and the collector is encouraged to buy a piece on its merit rather than its provenance, for all were seeking perfection.

The styles primarily associated with Nailsea are mottled metal and the festoon effect of one colour on another, or on clear glass. A good example will have clearly defined colours and regular festooning, as in Plate 119; a poor one will have weak colours and haphazard festoons. Walking-sticks, rolling-pins, pipes, flasks, and innumerable trinkets appeared in this ware in a number of colours, of which yellow is perhaps the least common. The metal is extremely varied, but there is more likelihood of Nailsea itself being the source if the metal has a tint of cloudy green; one should not regard the word 'Nailsea' (often in gilt) on the glass as conclusive evidence of its source, which may still be any one of ten or fifteen towns.

The industry in France during the early eighteenth century had made little progress, and importing was general. The Académie des Sciences perhaps mirrored the general concern of the French makers when in 1760 financial rewards were offered for suggestions to resuscitate the industry. The importance of this offer is probably overestimated and there are no grounds for connecting it with the establishment at Baccarat of a factory in 1765. This factory, which was subsequently to become celebrated as the Cristalleries de Baccarat, immediately introduced styles which approached the medium in a way different from the imports and copies that had flooded the French markets, and achieved the success that it has retained ever since.

The fame of Baccarat has been greatly enhanced by the paper-weights made there after about 1840, which can be divided into two distinct classes, *millefiori* and 'natural' weights, the former outnumbering the latter by at least two to one. The latter class, containing magnificent flowers, butterflies, snakes, and caterpillars, and the occasional salamander, is sufficiently rare to be a specialised subject; without the specialised know-ledge it is doubtful whether the collector will wish to pay the current prices. The former class is, however, still moderate in price by comparison and good *millefiori* weights change hands at prices well under fifty pounds. Most were made in the late 1840's and some carry the initial 'B' and a date (1848 is the most frequent, while the following year is, perhaps as the result of economic reconsideration, the rarest), the dated ones number-ing about 40 per cent of the total *millefiori* output. The date and initial will probably be found set in one of the many canes, in which may be seen any number of motifs. Of the *millefiori* weights the most sought after are generally the over-lay weights, which are themselves much rarer than many of the 'natural' weights. The overlay is cut to admit light and expose the *millefiori*, creating an effect which has an enduring fascination.

In the same period paper-weights were made at St Louis, whence come some of the finest weights featuring fruit and vegetables. *Millefiori* and floral effects are also made here, but the characteristics of the weights are different. Paul Jokelson, in his book *French Antique Paper-weights*, has dealt with the distinc-tions in detail, but it will suffice here to say that in general the effect and colouring of St Louis weights is softer than that of the Baccarat product and *millefiori* is used more as an incidental feature than as the main subject.

Clichy, the third centre famous for its weights, employed a somewhat more brilliant, clear metal, with the result that the colours themselves appear more brilliant. The predominant features are a rose and a swirling effect reminiscent of early *latticinio*, both of which were made well at Clichy; the *millefiori* weights are perhaps of a standard less uniformly high than those of Baccarat and St Louis, but are the staple product. Clichy weights are less varied than either of the other two types, but are sufficiently rare to provide the collector with a challenge.

Before we leave the subject of paper-weights, it is desirable that the would-be collector should realise that this is a field of collecting which sprang into sudden prominence in the 1950's, and because demand for antique paper-weights very soon exceeded supply, the prices for the genuine French weights have risen sharply. When the fashion for collecting paper-weights is at its height the inevitable mistakes of a beginner tend to be expensive.

Although Baccarat is particularly noted for its paper-weights, the other products of the glasshouse should not be neglected. Glass cutting, in styles of a less overwhelming nature than the English, and *crystallo-ceramie* were much practised arts by 1800, but it is in the field of shape that Baccarat excelled. If one discounts pieces made specifically for export, it is clear that the French retained some element of the elegance which in England was fast disappearing. The leading figure in France was Emile Gallé of Nancy (1846–1904), who turned back the pages and found that eerie quality of light and shade which had haunted *Waldglas*. Using an opaque metal (of modern standards, but having this eerie quality) and a tinted overlay, he achieved relief-work of a standard and peculiar beauty which none have since rivalled. Photography is unflattering to this particular form of glass, and the illustration (Plate 121) cannot catch the true value of the artistry. Although Gallé did not run his own glasshouse until 1875, he brought to the industry the eye of an artist and naturalist which he supplemented with the necessary technical skill to achieve the result he sought, a skill which came relatively easily to the son of a glassmaker who had been connected with the industry most of his life. Few modern artists have achieved his superb mastery of the metal, and perhaps the most genuine tribute to Gallé's greatness is the innumerable mass of copies, almost all inferior to the work of Gallé, which were made both during his life and after his death.

Moulded glass has of course been universally known since the earliest days of glass, but its production on a commercial scale does not appear to have achieved prominence again until the nineteenth century. It is probable that the art of press-moulding glass entered the New World in embryonic form, for the great name in the development of the art is that of the American Deming Jarves.

Jarves was a Boston man whose interest in glass led him to inventions which, perhaps more than the acts of any other man, consolidated the American industry. In 1821 he took out a patent for a machine which simplified the moulding operation, and a few years later he developed the technique of pressing glass in moulds, and protected his process with a series of patents. In 1825 he set up a glasshouse in Sandwich, and it is some measure of his success that even the heavily wooded area surrounding Sandwich could not satisfy his furnaces. Accordingly he took out a patent for a furnace, not dissimilar to that designed very much earlier in England, to enable him to use coal. By the time that this was perfected the Boston and Sandwich Glass Company was a really vast and prosperous concern; but Jarves himself had fallen out with his board over the problems of expansion, and in 1858, after ten years of fighting, he withdrew from the Company. It was a harsh blow from which Jarves, to whom his employees were devoted, never recovered.

The prosperity of the Company continued unabated, and Jarves's processes enabled the glasshouses to turn out a truly fantastic range and number of pieces. In December 1872 the output was assessed at 2,000 pieces per day; but the period of prosperity was drawing to a close, for labour disputes became frequent and ultimately crippled the Company in 1887.

The products of the Sandwich glasshouses are still numerous, and although press-moulded pieces are more frequent, there are fine examples of blowing and cutting and, less commonly, of pieces with specialised decoration. The metal is of a high standard and the colouring, which occurs in a wide variety of shades, is uniform in quality. As with all glass of this century, there remains the problem of distinguishing the original from the rivals' copies; and there is no doubt that Sandwich had many imitators, particularly of the dolphin-shaped objects (which achieved immediate popularity) and the lacework patterns that represent the peak of press-mould achievement in that century. This lacework could not possibly have been achieved by cutting, because of its intricacy, and was a completely new venture which attained lasting favour.

Another American achievement was the adoption of the styles initiated in France by Emile Gallé. Louis Tiffany (1848–1933) was among those who had studied under Gallé; and, although primarily interested in jewellery, he developed such a passion for glass that when he returned to New York he set up a glass-house and from 1892 onwards produced art-glass in which Gallé's inspiration is obvious. A further Tiffany technique was the spraying of the hot glass object with iron salt solution, which gave the object a metallic sheen. The name given to this process was 'Favrile', and the objects thus made have an appeal in which appreciation of glass as a metal has little part.

There is no doubt that America today produces pieces of glass which will in future years rank highly among antiques. The credit for this lies predominantly with one firm. In 1903 Frederick Carder (a glassmaker from Stourbridge who had worked under Northwood and Fabergé and had studied under Gallé, Lalique, and Tiffany) took over the Steuben Glassworks at Corning founded by Amory Houghton senior, and began to produce luxury art-glass. In 1918 the Steuben Glassworks were taken over by the larger Corning Glass Company, but were allowed to continue as before. The production of art-glass on a commercial basis requires the constant infusion of fresh talent, and this was not forthcoming until Amory Houghton junior in the 1930's revolutionised the Company's approach to art-glass. The finest artists were commissioned for some of the special pieces, and this policy has continued to the present day, with results that represent the finest in artistic achievement. John Piper, Matisse, and Jacob Epstein are only three of the vast number of internationally famous artists commissioned. When one considers that the Company has also produced a particularly fine quality metal, it is not difficult to envisage the esteem in which future generations must hold Steuben products. Naturally, with such a variety of talent, no distinctive characteristic runs through the range of products, except perhaps a certain impression of heaviness, an impression which is created by the deep lustre of the metal rather than the design.

The twentieth century has seen the emergence of national styles in various parts of the world, some of which have been noted for their glass in the past, some of which have only a very short history of production. It is not within the scope of this book to attempt even a summary of their achievements, and the reader is referred to the works set out in the Bibliography.

Bibliography

At the end of each chapter certain references are given which are not necessarily repeated here. Similarly titles appear here which are not mentioned elsewhere, the object of notes to the chapters being either to guide the reader to a general book on the subject from which further references may be obtained or to list works on specific subjects mentioned in the chapter.

AMIC, Y. *French Opaline Glasses of the 19th Century*, 1952.
ANGUS-BUTTERWORTH, L. M. *British Table and Ornamental Glass*, 1956.
ASH, DOUGLAS. *How to Identify English Drinking Glasses and Decanters 1680–1830*, 1961.
BARRELET, J. *La Verrerie en France*, 1955.
BATE, P. *English Tableglass*, 1905.
BEARD, G. W. *Cameo Glass—19th Century*, 1955.
BEDFORD, JOHN. *Bristol Coloured Glass*, 1964.
BERGSTRON, E. H. *Old Glass Paperweights*, 1947.
BLES, J. *Rare English Glasses of the 17th and 18th Centuries*, 1920.
BRINTON, W. *European Glass*, 1936.
BUCKLEY, FRANCIS. *A History of Old English Glass*, 1925.
BUCKLEY, WILFRED. *European Glass*, 1926.
—   *Frans Greenwood and his Engraved Glasses*, 1930.
CHAMBON, R. *History of Belgian Glass from the 2nd Century to the Present*, 1955.
CHARLESTON, R. J. *English Opaque White Glass – 18th Century*, 1962.
CHURCHILL, ARTHUR & CO. *Glass Notes.*
                    History in Glass, 1937.
CLARKE, H. G. *History of Old English Glass Pictures 1690–1810*, 1928.
DAVIS, DEREK. *English and Irish Antique Glass*, 1965.
DILLON, E. *History of Glass*, 1907.
EISEN, G. A. *Glass*, 2 vols., 1927.
ELVILLE, E. M. *English Tableglass*, 1951.
—   *English and Irish Cut Glass*, 1953.
—   *A Collector's Dictionary of Glass*, 1961.
—   *Paperweights and Other Glass Curiosities*, 1954.
FLEMING, A. *Scottish and Jacobite Glass*, 1938.
FOSSING, P. *Glass Vessels before Glassblowing*, 1940.
FRANCIS, G. R. *Old English Drinking Glasses*, 1926.
FROTHINGHAM, A. W. *Spanish Glass*, 1964.
—   *Barcelona Glass in Venetian Style*, 1956.
GASPARETTO, A. *Muranese Glass* (Italian Text), 1958.

GUTTERY, D. R. *From Broad-Glass to Cut Crystal*, 1956.
HARTSHORNE, A. *Old English Glasses*, 1897.
HAYNES, E. B. *Glass through the Ages*, 1948 (Revised 1959).
HETTES, KAREL. *Old Venetian Glass*, 1961.
HONEY, W. B. *English Glass*, 1946.
—   *Glass*, 1946.
HUGHES, G. BERNARD. *Table Glass in England, Scotland and Ireland*, 1956.
HUNTER, F. W. *Stiegel Glass*, N.D.
IMBERT AND AMIC. *French Crystal Paperweights*, 1948.
JENYNS AND WATSON. *Chinese Minor Arts*, 1964.
JOKELSON, P. *Antique French Paperweights*, 1955.
—   *100 of the most Important Paperweights*, 1966.
KOCH, R. *Tiffany Coloured Glass*, 1964.
LARSEN, RUSMOLTER AND SCHLUTER. *Danish Glass 1825–1925*, 1963.
LEE, R. W. *Early American Pressed Glass*, 1931.
LEWIS, J. S. *Old Glass and How to Collect It*, 1916.
MARIACHER, GIOVANNI. *Italian Blown Glass*, 1961.
MCKEARIN, H. AND G. S. *American Glass*, 1941.
—   *200 Years of American Blown Glass*, 1949.
MONSON-FITZJOHN, G. J. *Drinking Vessels of Bygone Days*, 1927.
MOORE, N. HUDSON. *Old Glass European and American*, 1926.
NERI, MERRET AND KUNCKEL. *Art de la Verrerie*, 1759.
NESBITT, A. *Glass Vessels of All Ages*, 1878.
NEUBERG, F. *Glass in Antiquity*, 1964.
—   *Ancient Glass*, 1962.
PARKER, J. E. *Asiatic Glassmaking* (Private Publication, 1937).
PELLATT, A. *Curiosities of Glassmaking*, 1849.
PELLIOT, M. *Verres Anciens*, 1929.
PERCIVAL, MACIVER. *The Glass Collector*, N.D.
PLAUT, J. S. *Steuben Glass*, 1948.
POLAK, ADA BUCH. *Gammelt Norsk Glass*, 1954.
POWELL, H. J. *Glassmaking in England*, 1923.
RAWSON, P. D. *Continental Glassmaking*, N.D.
RUGGLES-BRISE, S. *Sealed Bottles*, 1949.
SAVAGE, GEORGE. *Glass*, 1965.
SCHRIJVER, E. *Glass and Crystal*, 2 vols., 1963.
STANNUS, G. *Old Irish Glass*, 1920.
STEENBERG AND SIMMINGSKOLD. *Glas* (Swedish text), 1959.
THORPE, W. A. *A History of English and Irish Glass*, 2 vols., 1929.
—   *English Glass*, 1935.
—   *English and Irish Glass*, 1927.
VAVRA, J. *5000 Years of Glassmaking*, 1955.
WAKEFIELD, HUGH. *Nineteenth Century British Glass*, 1961.

WESTROPP, M. S. D. *Irish Glass*, 1920.
WILMER, D. *Early English Glass*, 1910.
WINBOLT, S. E. *Wealden Glass*, 1933.
YOXALL, J. H. *Collecting Old Glass*, 1916.

Further references:

A Bibliography of Glass, by George S. Duncan, 1960;
Journal of Glass Studies: produced by the Corning Museum of Glass;
Transactions of the Society of Glass Technology and *Transactions of the Glass Circle* (formerly *The Circle of Glass Collectors*).

Dates in the Development of English Glasses 1226–1825

1226	Laurence Vitrearius sets up a glasshouse at Dyer's Cross.
c. 1240	Laurence Vitrearius commissioned to make window-glass for Westminster Abbey.
1300	Chiddingfold receives the Royal Charter.
1343	The Schurterre family takes over the industry.
c. 1435	The Peytowe family becomes prominent.
1549	Carré comes to England.
1572	Carré dies.
1575	Verzelini is granted the monopoly on Venice Glasses.
1592	Verzelini retires. Bowes takes over.
1615	Proclamation prohibiting use of timber for fuel in furnaces. Mansell joins board of Zouche and Co.
1616	Death of Bowes.
1618	Mansell obtains sole control. Ravenscroft born.
1627	Mansell gains control of Hay's Scottish glasshouses.
1635	Glass Sellers' Company receives an unratified charter.
1656	Mansell dies.
1660	Restoration of Charles II. Buckingham assumes control of the industry.
1664	Valid charter granted to the Glass Sellers' Company.
1667–73	Greene's designs made in Murano.
1673	Ravenscroft sets up the Savoy glasshouse.
1674	Ravenscroft obtains his patent.
1675	Lead-glass introduced.
1677	The raven's head seal first used.
1681	Ravenscroft dies. Hawley Bishopp controls the Savoy glasshouse.
1685	Death of Charles II. Accession of James, Duke of York. Baluster period begins.
1688	James Francis Edward, the Old Pretender, born.
1689	William of Orange lands in England.
1690	Battle of the Boyne.
1695–9	20 per cent tax levied on glass.
1710	Foundation of the Cycle of the White Rose.
1714	Accession of George I.

1715   Moulded pedestal stem and balustroid stem period begins. First Jacobite rising.

1720   Charles Edward, the Young Pretender, born.

1725   Henry Benedict Stuart born. Baluster period closes. Plain stem dated period begins.

1735   Newcastle light baluster period begins. Air-twist stem period begins. Death of Maria Clementina Sobieska, wife of the Old Pretender.

1745   Second Jacobite rising. Opaque-twist stem, hollow stem, composite stem periods begin.

1746   Excise Act levies tax on the contents of the glass-pot.

1747   Henry Benedict Stuart becomes a cardinal.

1750   Incised twist, mixed twist, colour-twist, faceted stem periods begin.

1752   Charles Edward revisits London incognito.

1755   Moulded stem period closes.

1760   Balustroid, hollow stem, and incised twist periods close. Mercury-twist period begins. The Beilby family begin to enamel glass.

1765   Newcastle baluster period closes.

1766   Death of Old Pretender.

1770   Air-twist, mercury-twist, mixed twist and colour-twist periods close.

1775   Composite stem period closes.

1777   Excise Act doubles duty.

1780   Ireland obtains free trade. Opaque-twist period closes.

1788   Death of Young Pretender.

1810   Faceted stem period closes.

1821   Apsley Pellatt patents *crystallo-ceramie*.

1825   Irish glass taxed.

Index

*Printed in Great Britain
by W & J Mackay & Co Ltd, Chatham*